The Judgment of God

Randall Terry

The Reformer Library
Windsor, New York

To Rev. Rod Aguillard
Pastoral, Prophetic, Apostolic
One of the Finest and Rarest Men I Know

Printed in the United States of America
Unless otherwise noted, all Scripture quotations are from
the Holy Bible, New King James Version, ©1982 by Thomas
Nelson, Inc.
ISBN 1-887690-018

The Judgment
of God

CONTENTS

Part 1: The Ultimate Judge

    1. God is Judge / 3

Part 2: The Presence of Judgment

    2. Signs in the Sky / 11

    3. Striking the Breadbasket / 17

    4. The Plague / 21

    5. The Almighty Dollar / 27

    6. The Sword / 33

Part 3: The Reason for Judgment

    7. Why is Judgment Here? / 45

    8. What about the "Innocent"? / 61

    9. Does God Judge Nations? / 67

Part 4: The Warnings of Judgment

    10. Beware of False Prophets / 79

Part 5: The Aftermath of Judgment

    11. Survival of the Penitent / 93

    12. Rebuilding Our Nation / 109

Appendix: The Death of a Nation / 121

PART 1

The Ultimate Judge

1

GOD IS JUDGE

For we know Him who said, "Vengeance is Mine, I will repay," says the LORD. And again, "The LORD will judge His people." It is a fearful thing to fall into the hands of the living God.

Hebrews 10:30–31

CONTRARY TO POPULAR OPINION, God is not Santa Claus. The Almighty is not a jolly old perennial gift-giver, seeing who is naughty and nice, slipping in anonymously to dispense little toys for human happiness. Neither is the Ruler of the universe a semi-senile heavenly grandfather, who thinks everything His bratty grandchildren do is cute. Neither is he a Cosmic Watchmaker who set the universe in motion and then walked away.

God is the awesome, fearful, dread sovereign Lord of the universe to whom all men and nations will give an account. It matters not to Him whether we acknowledge

3

Him now, serve Him now or believe in Him now. He does not need our permission to be God. He *is* God.

And He is our Judge.

BELIEVERS' CONFUSION

Our problem in America is not with atheists or the pagans who are consistent with their unbelief, but with believers who are inconsistent with their belief. Millions of Americans believe in God but do not know or understand the God they believe in. Millions of professing Christians— those who have believed the Gospel and been baptized— view God as the foolish do, thinking, "'What does God know? Can He judge through the deep darkness?'" (Job 22:13).

Millions of believers lack wisdom, because they have lost the beginning of wisdom—the fear of God. The book of Proverbs states: "The fear of the LORD is the beginning of knowledge, but fools despise wisdom and instruction" (Proverbs 1:7).

What does the Bible say of this awesome God, the Judge of the world?

> O LORD God, to whom vengeance belongs—O God, to whom vengeance belongs, shine forth! Rise up, O Judge of the earth; render punishment to the proud. (Psalm 94:1–2)

> Thus says the LORD God to the land of Israel: "An end! The end has come upon the four corners of the land. Now the end *has come* upon you, and I will send My anger against you; I will judge you according to your ways, and I will repay you for all your abominations." (Ezekiel 7:1–3)

> The LORD shall judge the peoples; judge me, O LORD, according to my righteousness, and according to my

integrity within me. Oh, let the wickedness of the wicked come to an end, but establish the just; for the righteous God tests the hearts and minds. My defense is of God, who saves the upright in heart. God is a just judge, and God is angry with the wicked every day. (Psalm 7:8–11)

But the LORD shall endure forever; He has prepared His throne for judgment. He shall judge the world in righteousness, and He shall administer judgment for the peoples in uprightness. The LORD also will be a refuge for the oppressed, a refuge in times of trouble. And those who know Your name will put their trust in You; for You, LORD, have not forsaken those who seek You. When He avenges blood, He remembers them; He does not forget the cry of the humble. The LORD is known *by* the judgment He executes; the wicked is snared in the work of his own hands. Arise, O LORD, do not let man prevail; let the nations be judged in Your sight. Put them in fear, O LORD, that the nations may know themselves to be but men. (Psalm 9:7–10, 19–20)

The LORD *is* at Your right hand; He shall execute kings in the day of His wrath. He shall judge among the nations, He shall fill the places with dead bodies, He shall execute the heads of many countries. (Psalm 110:5–7)

"Vengeance is mine; I will repay," says the LORD. (Romans 12:19)

This is certainly not the image of the God of modern America. But this is the God of the Bible.

THE NATURE OF GOD

First John 4:16 states: "God is love." Millions of Americans—whether passionately or mindlessly—quote that glorious phrase, as if it were the whole essence and nature of God. But God is also "light" (see 1 John 1:5). He is "Spirit" (John 4:24), and most important to our discussion, "our God is a consuming fire" (Hebrews 12:29).

When we focus on one aspect of God's nature to the exclusion of other aspects of God's nature, we develop an out of balance, even a false, view of God. This is exactly what the proponents of the mush-love God have done. They have created a god in their own image: a god who tolerates all manner of wickedness; a god who embraces the latest moral fad; a god who would never punish a man, a woman, a family, or a nation for their sins. They have put forth a false god.

As we shall see, God does not allow His actions to be restrained or defined by His enemies, nor by confused, misguided armchair theologians. He is God. He is Judge. And He will pour out His judgments on a rebellious nation to get their attention, purge evil from their midst, and lead them back to the paths of righteousness.

THE JUDGMENT IS HERE

This book is based on two simple presuppositions: first, God exists; second, He has revealed Himself to us in the Holy Bible and *only* in the Holy Bible. To phrase it another way, *God is*, and *He has spoken*. These are the first principles on which Christendom builds its theology, its behavior, its philosophy, and its belief of the origin of the world.

This book presupposes that God is and that He is the Lord of all. I will not argue with the fool who rejects or denies the existence of God. I simply point him to the wonder and majesty of all creation, which testifies that God exists:

For since the creation of the world His invisible attributes are clearly seen, being understood by the things that are made, even His eternal power and Godhead, so that they are without excuse. (Romans 1:20)

I have read, watched, and listened—with humor and sadness—to the scorn and scathing rebukes I have received from newspaper columnists, television anchormen, and radio talk-show hosts because I have declared that the floods, the droughts, and plagues are the judgment of God. They refuse to accept a connection between national immorality and national calamity. They have ridiculed, belittled, dismissed, and in smug self-confidence sought to altogether ignore the clear teaching of the Bible on this matter.

On what do these scoffers base their beliefs? Their own opinion, perhaps? Their agnosticism? Their atheism? Their penchant for illicit sexual relations? Their "higher learning"?

I base my beliefs on the Ten Commandments, and on the teaching of the Bible. I base my view of the floods on the clear teachings of a sacred, inspired Book that has been with us for thousands of years: on a Book whose moral teachings and promise of salvation have brought peace to individuals, joy and longevity to families, and freedom and prosperity to nations.

When they mock or dismiss the teaching of the Scriptures, they are in fact saying that they are wiser than the Bible. They are declaring that we would be better off following their hollow, failed, self-centered ethical insanity written in two-bit newspapers, better off than taking a moral inventory and reforming our lives according to the teachings of the Bible.

Now I ask you: who is the fool here?

Whose words do you want to follow: Christ's or Dr. Ruth's? Whose law will you trust? Moses', or Bill and Hillary Clinton's? And upon whose precepts are you going to base your life and your view of the world: the Bible's or the latest *New York Times* poll?

I will take Christ, Moses, and the whole Bible any day of the week over all the combined folly and chaff of every newspaper editor, university professor, politician, or any other self-proclaimed fountain of wisdom who fancies themselves wiser than God's Word.

Let them mock. The Bible has been here for centuries. The above mentioned fools are the "new kid on the block." Christ and the Bible will still be the center of civilization long after their faithless lives have been forgotten.

> The voice said, "Cry out!" And he said, "What shall I cry?" "All flesh is grass, and all its loveliness is like the flower of the field. The grass withers, the flower fades, because the breath of the LORD blows upon it; surely the people are grass. The grass withers, the flower fades, But the word of our God stands forever." (Isaiah 40:6-8)

How does God judge a nation? He has many means at His disposal. In the beginning, judgment might be only annoying to many Americans. If we remain stiff-necked, however, in the end His judgments will be catastrophic and terrifying, threatening our very survival as a nation.

How bad will it get? That depends on when we get the message that God is not pleased with our selfishness, and turn back to Him as a nation. First, we need to examine the judgments He is using and will yet use to bring us back to moral sanity.

PART 2

The Presence of Judgment

2

SIGNS IN THE SKY

I will break the pride of your power; I will make
your heavens like iron and your earth like bronze.

Leviticus 26:19

S EARING DROUGHTS IN SOUTH CAROLINA
and Georgia. Relentless flooding in the Midwest.
Devastating hurricanes in Florida and Hawaii. Suffocating blizzards in the Northeast. Fires in the West.

New Agers claim it is mother nature. Agnostics assure us it's chance. Confused Christians blame the devil.

They are all wrong.

The Bible teaches clearly that the weather is in the hand of God:

When He utters His voice, there is a multitude of
waters in the heavens: "And He causes the vapors

to ascend from the ends of the earth. He makes lightning for the rain. He brings the wind out of His treasuries." (Jeremiah 10:13)

Are there any among the idols of the nations that can cause rain? Or can the heavens give showers? Are You not He, O LORD our God? Therefore we will wait for You, Since You have made all these. (Jeremiah 14:22)

God causes it to rain on the just and the unjust (see Matthew 5:45). God uses the rain and the sun to bestow blessing on mankind and the whole earth:

Then I will give you the rain for your land in its season, the early rain and the latter rain, that you may gather in your grain, your new wine, and your oil. And I will send grass in your field for your livestock, that you may eat and be filled. (Deuteronomy 11:14–15)

Sing to the LORD with thanksgiving; sing praises on the harp to our God, Who covers the heavens with clouds, Who prepares rain for the earth, Who makes grass to grow on the mountains. (Psalm 147:7–8)

And just as the weather is in the hand of God to bless us, it is in His hand to chasten us for our sins. The Scripture says:

"I also withheld rain from you, when there were still three months to the harvest. I made it rain on one city, I withheld rain from another city. One part was rained upon, and where it did not rain the part withered. So two or three cities wandered to another city to drink water, but they were not satisfied; yet you have not returned to Me," says the LORD. (Amos 4:7–8)

God clearly warns that if we persist in our rebellion:

And your heavens which are over your head shall be bronze, and the earth which is under you shall be iron. The LORD will change the rain of your land to powder and dust; from the heaven it shall come down on you until you are destroyed. (Deuteronomy 28:23–24)

Or He may choose to use floods:

He who builds His layers in the sky, and has founded His strata in the earth; who calls for the waters of the sea, and pours them out on the face of the earth—the LORD is His name. (Amos 9:6)

Also with moisture He saturates the thick clouds; He scatters His bright clouds. And they swirl about, being turned by His guidance, that they may do whatever He commands them on the face of the whole earth. He causes it to come, whether for correction, or for His land, or for mercy. (Job 37:11–13)

"But wait!" someone will say. "God promised Noah He would never again destroy the earth by flood!"

That is correct. And He has kept and will keep that promise. He is not destroying the earth by flood. He has just chastened one small area with excessive water. (We will deal with good people who lost their farms in chapter 7). His prophets have warned that His judgment will come. And at times the people cannot prevent it from happening. They are given this direction:

Seek the LORD, all you meek of the earth, who have upheld His justice. Seek righteousness, seek humility. It may be that you will be hidden in the day of the LORD's anger. (Zephaniah 2:3)

Some will be tempted to view God as an ogre at this point, as a divine being who has had a bad day and suddenly lashes out at us as if we were ants and grasshoppers. Not so.

Why does God judge us? Amos 4:8 holds the key: "'Yet you have not returned to Me,' says the LORD." When God chastens us, it is so that we will return to Him as a nation. He sends storms "for correction" (Job 37:13). Sometimes His chastenings are a token of His love: "For whom the LORD loves He chastens" (Hebrews 12:6).

Sometimes He puts us flat on our backs so the only place we can look is heavenward.

Because they rebelled against the words of God, and despised the counsel of the Most High, therefore He brought down their heart with labor; they fell down, and there was none to help. Then they cried out to the LORD in their trouble, and He saved them out of their distresses. He brought them out of darkness and the shadow of death, and broke their chains in pieces. Oh, that men would give thanks to the LORD for His goodness, and for His wonderful works to the children of men! (Psalm 107:11–15)

And we must understand that His power is limitless. If America does not respond to the first-fruits of judgment—as we have not—God has much more calamity at His disposal to break our rebellion. Or put another way, God has more disaster than the U. S. Government has relief.

God has hail:

Have you entered the treasury of snow, or have you seen the treasury of hail, which I have reserved for the time of trouble, for the day of battle and war? (Job 22–23)

God has more blistering droughts:

A drought is against her waters, and they will be dried up. For it is the land of carved images, and they are insane with their idols. (Jeremiah 50:38)

God has hurricanes:

You will be punished by the LORD of hosts with thunder and earthquake and great noise, with storm and tempest and the flame of devouring fire. (Isaiah 29:6)

God has more earthquakes:

Then the earth shook and trembled; the foundations of the hills also quaked and were shaken, because He was angry. (Psalm 18:7)

God has more lightning to start wildfires:

Upon the wicked He will rain coals; fire and brimstone and a burning wind shall be the portion of their cup. (Psalm 11:6)

Praise the LORD from the earth, you great sea creatures and all the depths; fire and hail, snow and clouds; stormy wind, fulfilling His word. (Psalm 148:7–8)

God has floods:

> Also I will make justice the measuring line, and righteousness the plummet; the hail will sweep away the refuge of lies, and the waters will overflow the hiding place. (Isaiah 28:17).

In all reality, while the weather chastenings we have experienced have brought great hardship to many thousands and even death to a few (and for those thus bereaved we should grieve), the vast majority of America hasn't even skipped a beat because of these preliminary wake up calls. We continue ignoring God, blaming random chance or ozone thinning or foreign volcanoes, or Kuwait's fires for our troubles. We will not acknowledge that God rules the elements.

This does not bode well for us. God will continue to call to us and rebuke us through nature and signs in the sky. Then He will move on the other means of judgment He has promised in His Word and used throughout history. It will not be pleasant.

3

STRIKING THE BREADBASKET

When I have cut off your supply of bread, ten women shall bake your bread in one oven, and they shall bring back to you your bread by weight, and you shall eat and not be satisfied.

Leviticus 26:26

THE PHYSICAL HEALTH AND WELL-BEING of mankind is inseparably linked with food. When our nutrition is poor, our bodies break down. If our nutrition intake ceases, so will our very lives. With poor food, we will suffer; with no food, we will die.

America's breadbasket has been filled beyond measure for most of her history. Massive crop failure has occurred at points in the past, and the Great Depression was a time when millions were unsure where their daily bread would come from. But for the most part, very few Americans have ever known hunger. The vast amount of food stuffs we have produced literally staggers the mind. America's abundant food supply is a testament of God's blessing (see Isaiah 9:3, Matthew 6:11, and Acts 14:17).

But just like the weather, what God holds in His hand for blessing He can also use for cursing. He can bless our crops or curse them. He can multiply our herds or send them ravaging disease and miscarrying wombs. God said:

"I blasted you with blight and mildew. When your gardens increased, your vineyards, your fig trees, and your olive trees, the locust devoured them; yet you have not returned to Me," says the LORD. (Amos 4:9)

Therefore the LORD God of hosts, the LORD, says this: "There shall be wailing in all streets, and they shall say in all the highways, 'Alas! Alas!' They shall call the farmer to mourning, and skillful lamenters to wailing." (Amos 5:16)

God spells out the agricultural disaster that awaits the nation that rebels against Him:

You shall plant vineyards and tend them, but you shall neither drink of the wine nor gather the grapes; for the worms shall eat them. You shall have olive trees throughout all your territory, but you shall not anoint yourself with the oil; for your olives shall drop off. Locusts shall consume all your trees and the produce of your land. (Deuteronomy 28:39–40, 42)

For they shall eat, but not have enough; they shall commit harlotry, but not increase; because they have ceased obeying the LORD. (Hosea 4:10)

"I struck you with blight and mildew and hail in all the labors of your hands; yet you did not turn to Me," says the LORD. (Haggai 2:17)

Along with destruction of our crops and livestock, we would do well to notice the increase of wild animals bearing diseases. For example, rabies was thought all but extinct. Now an epidemic has broken out in some states, claiming not only thousands of animals, but several people as well.

The Bible says:

They shall be wasted with hunger, devoured by pestilence and bitter destruction; I will also send against them the teeth of beasts, with poison of serpents of the dust. (Deuteronomy 32:24)

"And I will appoint over them four forms of destruction ,"says the LORD: "the sword to slay, the dogs to drag, the birds of the heavens and the beasts of the earth to devour and destroy." (Jeremiah 15:3)

"I will send wild beasts among you, which shall rob you of your children, destroy your livestock, and make you few in number." (Leviticus 26:22)

A few drought areas and a couple of bad years of crops are not going to cripple the United States of America. However, when enough crops fail and when herds die, a genuine famine can ensue. Severe malnutrition and even starvation—breadbasket chastening taken to its extreme—are a real threat from heaven against a rebellious nation. If our nation persists in its rebellion God has more severe means of breaking our rebellious spirit. And as we shall see, if we yet will not bow the knee, God can combine His judgments in such a way that the final end is nothing short of gruesome.

4

THE PLAGUE

"I also will do this to you: I will even appoint terror over you, wasting disease and fever which shall consume the eyes and cause sorrow of heart."

Leviticus 26:17a

M ANY OF US GREW UP hearing the expression, "If you don't have your health, you don't have anything." While this axiom is overstated, the truth remains that good health is an indescribably wondrous blessing. Most people have been laid low at least once or twice in their lives with some virus; most have endured violent nausea or uncontrollable trembling from hot and cold flashes. Those brief encounters with sickness serve to make people appreciate good health all the more.

Many people have also endured the agonizing experience of watching a loved one slowly die, of seeing a beloved friend waste away and finally depart from this world. It can be heart-wrenching—even when they possess the unshakable faith that their loved one has gone to heaven.

Sickness and, without fail, death are the unwanted companions of all the living. And so this topic is all the more painful to explore. We have too often sealed an obtuse theological debate with our own anguish. But private pain cannot be allowed to skew truth. And wishful thinking cannot be allowed to warp divine reality.

For the truth is that sometimes God sends plagues among a nation to judge them. God says that clearly, "I sent among you a plague after the manner of Egypt" (Amos 4:10). The Bible offers many examples:

- When Pharaoh refused to let the Israelites go, God struck the whole nation with boils (see Exodus 9:8–11).

- When Pharaoh persisted in his rebellion, God smote the first-born of all Egypt (see Exodus 12:29–30).

- When the Philistine had taken the sacred ark of the covenant—the earthly throne of God—and put it in the temple of their pagan idol Dagon, God ultimately struck the whole nation with tumors (see 1 Samuel 5:9).

- When the children of Israel sinned against the Lord, He sent a plague among them (see Numbers 16:46–50).

- When King Uzziah went into the temple to burn incense to the Lord—contrary to the Law of God—God struck him with leprosy (see 2 Chronicles 26:16–21).

- When Nabal reviled David in the wilderness, God struck him so that he died (see 1 Samuel 25:36–38).

- When David committed adultery with Bathsheba
and had Uriah murdered, God took the life of the
child of David's adulterous union (see 2 Samuel
11:2—12:23).

It is an inescapable theme of the Bible that God uses
sickness to discipline men and nations.

BY HIS STRIPES, WE ARE HEALED

Let me hasten to say, God has declared, "I am the LORD
that heals you" (Exodus 15:26).

Jesus Christ frequently healed the sick and/or set them
free from demons that caused sickness (see for example
Matthew 9:27–33, 12:22, 15:28, 17:14–18; Mark 1:26, 34,
7:31–37, 9:25; Luke 8:2, 9:39,42, 11:14, 13:11–17, John
4:46–54). I believe God still heals people today. He is the
same yesterday, today, and forever. He never changes. (See
Hebrews 13:8 and James 1:17.)

But nevertheless, the God who has the power to send
pleasant rain or devastating drought, the God who can
multiply our produce or send locusts to devour it, the God
who blesses families and nations with good health can also
strip them of the health to inspire them to reform their
ways.

Many Christians in America foolishly believe and teach
others that God never makes anyone sick, that only the
devil makes people sick, and hence, all disease is from
Satan. But as we have seen from Scriptures, God can and
does make people sick to chasten or judge them. New
Testament passages also confirm the Old Testament verses.
Saint Paul taught that when some early Christians had
partaken of communion "unworthily" they became sick,
some even died:

> For he who eats and drinks in an unworthy manner
> eats and drinks judgment to himself, not discerning
> the LORD's body. For this reason many are weak and
> sick among you, and many sleep. (1 Corinthians
> 11:29–30)

Likewise, Jesus Himself threatened sickness and even death to a rebellious unrepentant faction in the church of Thyatira:

> Nevertheless I have a few things against you, because
> you allow that woman Jezebel, who calls herself a
> prophetess, to teach and seduce My servants to com-
> mit sexual immorality and eat things sacrificed to
> idols. And I gave her time to repent of her sexual
> immorality, and she did not repent. Indeed I will cast
> her into a sickbed, and those who commit adultery
> with her into great tribulation, unless they repent of
> their deeds. (Revelation 2:20–22)

Does that mean that all sickness comes from God as a result of sin in someone's life? In other words if someone is sick, is God punishing that person?

Absolutely not. Jesus Himself answered that question when the religious leaders of His day asked Him. (See John 9:1-3.)

To be honest, this is an area that we see through a glass darkly. We know that at times the devil has made people sick. We know that God has sent sickness and plagues. We also know that if people go outside for too long in the winter without a coat, they will catch a cold and that cold could turn to pneumonia without proper care.

My point? I don't believe there is a pat answer that explains every sickness in every individual. We must look at each situation first in the light of God's Word, and then the individual's or nation's experience.

Death Has Climbed Through Our Windows

In the light of the Holy Bible and in view of our nation's state of moral anarchy, I have come to the conclusion that A.I.D.S. is the judgment of God. I could be wrong, but I believe this horrifying plague is the chastening of the Lord against our nation as a whole and against the homosexual lifestyle in particular.

The thought of A.I.D.S. being a judgment from the Almighty might violate every concept of God you have ever had. You may ask, how could a God of love send such a disease? The answer is because He is also just. And holy. And righteous. Romans 1:26–28 says:

> For this reason God gave them up to vile passions. For even their women exchanged the natural use for what is against nature. Likewise also the men, leaving the natural use of the woman, burned in their lust for one another, *men with men committing what is shameful, and receiving in themselves the penalty of their error which was due.* And even as they did not like to retain God in their knowledge, God gave them over to a debased mind, to do those things which are not fitting. (emphasis added)

Moreover, like all divine punishments, a plague may be a token of mercy to us. If A.I.D.S. is part of what it takes to call this nation to repentance, if A.I.D.S. will jolt us out of the perverse and evil behaviors that have brought us this crisis, it is a kindness from heaven to us. And certainly, A.I.D.S. isn't the only health crisis on the horizon. Other frightening diseases, viruses, strains, etc., have cropped up and may yet crop up.

You may also ask, but what about the innocent! What about innocent little babies who have A.I.D.S.! I know. It is horrifying. I will deal with this question in detail shortly in chapter 8. But let me say this: No man lives to himself, and no man dies to himself. The horrifying truth is that irresponsible or wicked behavior can harm or kill innocent people—whether through drunk driving or the spread of A.I.D.S.

We cannot claim that a plague is unjust or unfair. The Bible warns us of the fierce judgments that await a nation that rebels against Him and resists His call to reform.

> The LORD will make the plague cling to you until He has consumed you from the land which you are going to possess. The LORD will strike you with consumption, with fever, with inflammation, with severe burning fever, with the sword, with scorching, and with mildew; they shall pursue you until you perish. (Deuteronomy 28:21–22)

> The LORD will strike you with the boils of Egypt, with tumors, with the scab, and with the itch, from which you cannot be healed. The LORD will strike you with madness and blindness and confusion of heart. (Deuteronomy 28:27–28)

> I also will do this to you: I will even appoint terror over you, wasting disease and fever which shall consume the eyes and cause sorrow of heart. (Leviticus 26:16)

The Bible could not be clearer. Plagues are a part of the judgment of God.

If however, fatal scourges are not enough to turn our hearts—as so far they have not—God is able to judge us in a way that He will surely gain *all* our attention. God will strike our wallets.

5

THE ALMIGHTY DOLLAR

*And the LORD will grant you plenty of goods, in the
fruit of your body, in the increase of your livestock,
and in the produce of your ground, in the land of
which the LORD swore to your fathers to give you.
You shall lend to many nations, but you shall not
borrow. And the LORD will make you the head and
not the tail; you shall be above only, and not be
beneath, if you heed the commandments of the
LORD your God, which I command you today, and
are careful to observe them.*

Deuteronomy 28:11–13

T HE UNITED STATES OF AMERICA has been the
most financially prosperous nation in the history of
mankind. This is undoubtedly due to the blessing of God.

But the God who prospered us and enabled us to climb
to dizzying economic heights has the clear ability—and
stated intentions—of flicking us off our precipice like an

annoyed farmer flicks a fly off the top of a pitchfork. Read the following passages:

> Now therefore, thus says the LORD of hosts: "Consider your ways! You have sown much, and bring in little; you eat, but do not have enough; you drink, but you are not filled with drink; you clothe yourselves, but no one is warm; and he who earns wages, earns wages to put into a bag with holes." (Haggai 1:5–6)

> "And you shall grope at noonday, as a blind man gropes in darkness; you shall not prosper in your ways; you shall not dwell in it; you shall be only oppressed and plundered continually, and no one shall save you." (Deuteronomy 28:29)

> And your strength shall be spent in vain; for your land shall not yield its produce, nor shall the trees of the land yield their fruit. (Leviticus 26:20)

The following passage sounds like a report from the *Wall Street Journal:*

> The alien who is among you shall rise higher and higher above you, and you shall come down lower and lower. He shall lend to you, but you shall not lend to him; he shall be the head, and you shall be the tail. (Deuteronomy 28:43–44)

America used to be the world's largest lender nation; now we are the world largest debtor nation. The British, the Dutch, the Japanese, and others are rising higher and higher in our midst as we sink lower and lower. God is able to humble us in poverty before our foreign nations—whether friend or foe.

Because you did not serve the LORD your God with
joy and gladness of heart, for the abundance of everything, therefore you shall serve your enemies, whom
the LORD will send against you, in hunger, in thirst,
in nakedness, and in need of everything; and He will
put a yoke of iron on your neck until He has destroyed
you. (Deuteronomy 28:47–48)

In Nehemiah's day, the Israelites were punished for
their idolatry, and their chastening included the surrender
of their wealth.

Here we are, servants today! And the land that You
gave to our fathers, to eat its fruit and its bounty, here
we are, servants in it! And it yields much increase to
the kings You have set over us, because of our sins;
also they have dominion over our bodies and our
cattle at their pleasure; and we are in great distress.
(Nehemiah 9:36–37)

Jeremiah's warning should be heeded today.

O My mountain in the field, I will give as plunder your
wealth, all your treasures, and your high places of sin
with all your borders. And you, even yourself, shall let
go of your heritage which I gave you; and I will cause
you to serve your enemies in the land which you do
not know; for you have kindled a fire in My anger
which shall burn forever. (Jeremiah 17:3–4)

And God still has the power to make us economic
slaves—as we are fast becoming—if we continue to rebel
against Him.

There is one more contemporary reason why our economy is slated for calamity. Wealth—which can be a blessing
from God used for His glory—has become an idol in our

midst. Money has become a false god to millions of Americans.

Just as the bronze serpent that Moses and Aaron held up by the wilderness for healing ultimately became an idol that God destroyed (see Numbers 21), even so the United States' economy—which has brought blessing to so many millions at home and overseas—has become a golden calf, an idol fit for destruction.

Let me be more precise. I believe the country at large and the Christian community in particular may have sped our economy toward God's judgment when they rallied behind Bill Clinton in the 1992 election. Mr. Clinton made it absolutely clear that he would push for more abortion, more homosexuality, more condoms to teenagers—yet millions of professing Christians voted for him anyway.

Why? Was it his soft eyes? Was it that lower lip strategically bit when the reporters questioning got too hot? Was it his wife? No, it was *money*—plain and simple.

Bill Clinton promised more money and more goodies. And Christians and non-Christians alike religiously ignored Clinton's clearly stated immoral agenda and voted for the promise of more money. (What a joke *that* turned out to be!)

Let me say it another way: Christians sold out. They put money ahead of the clear Word of God. They bowed to a silver idol. They worshipped a golden calf. They knelt at the throne of the almighty dollar. They voted for a man who promised more money—and squared his promises for more dead babies and sodomy "rights."

And God is not pleased. In fact, God has a habit of smashing idols (see 1 Samuel 5). Scripture says, ". . . the LORD Himself is God, there is none other besides Him" (Deuteronomy 4:35). And the idol of "the economy" is no exception. Our economy is going to crash with such calamity that it could make the Great Depression look like a boom economy. The financial turmoil will be so severe that the "best" and "wisest" so-called "financial experts" will wring their hands in dismay.

Hyper-inflation, the collapse of the dollar, massive unemployment, the failures of huge banking institutions are all on the horizon. God is bigger than our schemes, greater than the Federal Deposit Insurance Corporation, smarter than the Federal Reserve, and more powerful than banking cartels. He will humble us in what was once our glory.

Our money may say "In God We Trust," but God is not impressed. He wants genuine obedience, not shallow cliches.

If, however, we still do not get the message, if we persist in our defiance of the Ten Commandments as a nation, God can resort to the ultimate earthly judgment; the sword.

6

THE SWORD

"Your ways and your doing have procured these things for you. This is your wickedness, because it is bitter, because it reaches to your heart."

Jeremiah 4:18

A MERICA'S TWO-HUNDRED-PLUS year history has been graced with an incredible legacy of domestic peace and stability. Our borders have not been breached by a foreign power since the war of 1812; until recently, our cities were among the safest in the world. People went to bed with their doors unlocked. They felt secure knowing that their children were playing "somewhere in the neighborhood."

The stability and peace we once enjoyed, as well as international military stature, were part of the blessing of God.

> I will give peace in the land, and you shall lie down,
> and none will make you afraid; I will rid the land of
> evil beasts, and the sword will not go through your
> land. You will chase your enemies, and they shall fall
> by the sword before you. (Leviticus 26:6–7)

But like all the other blessings that we have taken for
granted or foolishly believed while saying in our hearts
". . . 'My power and the might of my hand have gained me
this wealth'" (Deuteronomy 8:17), the blessing of peace
and safety is being wrenched from our grasp.

Everything is changing. The sword has begun to fall.

God is handing us over to violence. As we shall see, the
sword can take the face of many acts of cruelty or barbarism, whether random violence in our cities, gang wars,
terrorism, civil war, defeat in the field of battle, or conquest
and occupation from a foreign foe.

Many historic sections of our cities, well known for
vibrant local culture, have been devastated.

God says:

> How the faithful city has become a harlot! It was full
> of justice; righteousness lodged in it, but now mur-
> derers. Your silver has become dross, your wine
> mixed with water. Your princes are rebellious, and
> companions of thieves; everyone loves bribes, and
> follows after rewards. They do not defend the father-
> less, nor does the cause of the widow come before
> them. (Isaiah 1:21–23)

How does He avenge this wickedness?

> Therefore the LORD says, the LORD of hosts, the
> Mighty One of Israel, "Ah, I will rid Myself of My
> adversaries, and take vengeance on My enemies, I will
> turn My hand against you, and thoroughly purge

away your dross, and take away all your alloy." (Isaiah 1:24–25)

I will lay your cities waste and bring your sanctuaries to desolation, and I will not smell the fragrance of your sweet aromas. (Leviticus 26:31)

The lion has come up from his thicket, and the destroyer of nations is on his way. He has gone forth from his place to make your land desolate. Your cities will be laid waste, without inhabitant. For this, clothe yourself with sackcloth, lament and wail. For the fierce anger of the LORD has not turned back from us. (Jeremiah 4:7–8)

Whole sections of major urban areas that were once alive and safe look like Beruit. Our cities are slowly being laid waste before our eyes. This is the fruit of a nation that has turned its back on God.

GANGS

As a nation, we have rejected God's Law concerning the sacredness of marriage; we have tried to redefine God's pattern for family and family duties. God is angry. And we are reaping as God's Word warned:

"I will give children to be their princes, and babes shall rule over them. The people will be oppressed, every one by another and every one by his neighbor; the child will be insolent toward the elder, and the base toward the honorable. Woe to the wicked! It shall be ill with him, for the reward of his hands shall be given him. As for My people, children are their oppressors ..." (Isaiah 3:4–5,11–12)

In hundreds of our communities, the elderly do not dare leave their homes at certain times for fear of disrespectful, violent youths. This is the fruit of our rejection of God's Laws. God is handing us over to violence.

TERRORISM

Terrorism is potent, a fearful punishment against a nation that has rejected Him.

> "Your ox shall be slaughtered before your eyes, but you shall not eat of it; your donkey shall be violently taken away from before you, and shall not be restored to you; your sheep shall be given to your enemies, and you shall have no one to rescue them." (Deuteronomy 28:31)

> ". . . and if you despise my statutes, or if your soul abhors my judgments, so that you do not perform all my commandments, *but* break My covenant. I also will do this to you: I will even appoint terror over you, wasting disease and fever which shall consume the eyes and cause sorrow of heart. And I will bring a sword against you that will execute the vengeance of *My* covenant; when you are gathered together within your cities I will send pestilence among you; and you shall be delivered into the hand of the enemy. (Leviticus 26:15–16a, 25)

The Muslim threat of terrorism is looming larger on the horizon. God has thousands of middle-east radicals at His disposal, men who passionately hate America. As God lifts His providential protecting hand from us and hands us over to the sword, what can we expect?

> "The LORD will bring a nation against you from afar, from the end of the earth, as swift as the eagle flies, a nation whose language you will not understand, 'a nation of fierce countenance, which does not respect

the elderly nor show favor to the young.'" (Deuteronomy 28:49–50)

And obviously, God does not have to raise up foreign adversaries to strike terror in our hearts. The seeds of destruction can come from our own souls.

". . . Pestilence and blood shall pass through you, and I will bring the sword against you. I, the LORD, have spoken. (Ezekiel 5:17)

CIVIL WAR

This nation has already experienced one horrifying civil war. I have no doubt that it was the judgment of God against us for participating in, and tolerating the unjust and oppressive slavery in our midst. Do you think those are the words of a misguided extremist? Read the words of another misguided extremist, Abraham Lincoln:

If we shall suppose that American slavery is one of those offenses which, in the providence of God, must needs come, but which, having continued through His appointed time, He now wills to remove, and that He gives to both North and South this terrible war as the woe due to those by whom the offense came, shall we discern therein any departure from those divine attributes which the believers in a living God always ascribe to Him? Fondly do we hope, fervently do we pray, that this mighty scourge of war may speedily pass away. Yet, if God wills that it continue until all the wealth piled into the bondsman's two hundred and fifty years of unrequited toil shall be sunk, and until every drop of blood drawn with the lash shall be paid by another drawn with the sword, as was said three thousand years ago, so still it must be said "the judgments of the Lord are true and righteous altogether."

It is rather remarkable that our sixteenth president not only believed, but freely expressed his belief in a God who brings wrath on a wicked country—*our* country. Were he alive today, the perfectly manicured, plaster-of-Paris make-up television anchors would laugh him to scorn. I long for the days when we once again have godly statesmen serving and leading our nation instead of ungodly, cowardly politicians furthering their own careers. The Lord promised ancient Israel this would happen. And certainly the principle would apply to us if we will repent.

> "I will restore your judges as at the first, and your counselors as at the beginning, afterward you shall be called the city of righteousness, the faithful city." (Isaiah 1:26)

DEFEAT IN BATTLE

Another stage in the judgment of the sword is defeat in battle. The war with Iraq was a great military success for the United States. But the war in Vietnam was a humiliating defeat. We were disgraced in Beirut and in Somalia. Do more Vietnams, Beiruts, and Somalias await us on the field of battle?

> ". . . your young men I killed with a sword, along with your captive horses; I made the stench of your camps come up into your nostrils; yet you have not returned to Me," says the LORD. (Amos 4:10)

> The LORD will cause you to be defeated before your enemies; you shall go out one way against them and flee seven ways before them; and you shall become troublesome to all the kingdoms of the earth. Your carcasses shall be food for all the birds of the air and the beasts of the earth, and no one shall frighten them away." (Deuteronomy 28:25–26)

Enemy Occupation

Perhaps the worst form of earthly judgment that God could bring against a nation is the defeat, occupation, and even the destruction of that nation by a foreign enemy.

God is fully able to bring this horrifying judgment upon us.

> And I will bring you out of its midst, and deliver you into the hands of strangers, and execute judgments on you. You shall fall by the sword. I will judge you at the border of Israel, then you shall know that I am the LORD. (Ezekiel 11:9–10)

Throughout history He has judged nations. The seven Canaanite Nations of antiquity had become so vile and corrupt before God that His intention was to obliterate them.

> When the LORD your God brings you into the land which you go to possess, and has cast out many nations before you, the Hittites and the Girgashites and the Amorites and the Canaanites and the Perizzites and the Hivites and the Jebusites, seven nations greater and mightier than you, and when the LORD your God delivers them over to you, you shall conquer them and utterly destroy them. You shall make no covenant with them nor show mercy to them. For they will turn your sons away from following Me, to serve other gods; so the anger of the LORD will be aroused against you and destroy you suddenly. But thus you shall deal with them: you shall destroy their altars, and break down their sacred pillars, and cut down their wooden images, and burn their carved images with fire. (Deuteronomy 7:1–2, 4–5)

In ancient Israel, after civil war (another judgment from God) had divided the country, the Ten Northern

Tribes became so corrupt that God handed them over to the Assyrians to be defeated in battle and scattered throughout two continents. Their nation was never rebuilt.

I realize the thought of a foreign enemy occupying the United States is absurd to most of us now. But before the Nazi blitzkrieg of 1939, France was believed to have had the greatest army on earth. In 1936, the thought of Germany conquering France was inconceivable. Times change.

Also consider Israel and the prophet Amos. When Amos prophesied the destruction of Israel—drought, famine, plague, the sword—Israel was in a state of great wealth and prosperity. Her enemies, the Syrians and the Assyrians, were in disarray and not a threat to her security.

Amos' predictions of military conquest must have seemed laughable then, too. But before fifty years had elapsed, the Assyrians came and obliterated the Ten Northern Tribes in a crushing military conquest. The conquerors scattered their survivors to the wind and transplanted other pagan peoples into the land of Israel (from whence came the despised Samaritans). Israel never recovered from this fatal blow. (See 2 Kings: 17, Amos, and Hosea.)

We are fools if we think that our current prosperity, our military standing in the world, and the current disarray of many of our enemies, makes us as safe as an eagle in a mountain crag. If Almighty God decrees our disaster, all the patriot missiles and stealth bombers in the world could not protect us from defeat at the hands of our enemies. God will aid our enemies in our defeat just as surely as He brought down the impenetrable walls of Jericho so that the Israelites would destroy them.

Furthermore, even if we never are invaded by an enemy force, the forces of terrorism—foreign and domestic—can continue to raise their horrifying head. The first bitter fruits of violence we have sown are being eaten in our land and yet it seems very few recognize the law of God at work—the law of sowing and reaping. We have sowed violence and oppression as a nation, and we are beginning to reap the rancid fruit.

When will we see the direct connection between our rebellion to God as a nation, and His outpoured judgments?

Part 3

The Reason for Judgment

7

WHY IS JUDGMENT HERE?

*And He gave them into the hand of the Gentiles,
and those who hated them ruled over them. Their
enemies also oppressed them, and they were
brought into subjection under their hand.*

Psalm 106:41–42

B Y NOW YOU SHOULD BE WONDERING, "Exactly *what* have we done wrong to earn the ire of Heaven? What are our specific sins that have provoked God to pour out judgment upon us?"

America is guilty before God for many sins; in particular, the shedding of innocent blood, homosexuality and sexual perversion, and blasphemy.

THE SHEDDING OF INNOCENT BLOOD

Of all the crimes men commit against each other, this is the most heinous. Bloodshed is a higher crime than other sins in the Bible, which is one of the reasons murder is a capital offense.

Blood talks to God. It cries to Him from the ground. When Cain killed Abel, God said to Cain: "... The voice of your brother's blood cries out to Me from the ground" (Genesis 4:10).

After the flood, the only negative command God had was about bloodshed.

> "Surely for your lifeblood I will demand a reckoning; from the hand of every beast I will require it, and from the hand of man. From the hand of every man's brother I will require the life of man. Whoever sheds man's blood, by man his blood shall be shed. . . ." (Genesis 9:4–6)

In Psalm 106:34–35 there is the direct connection between shedding innocent blood and the destruction of a nation:

> They even sacrificed their sons and their daughters to demons, and shed innocent blood, even the blood of their sons and daughters, whom they sacrificed to the idols of Canaan; and the land was polluted with blood. Thus they were defiled by their own works, and played the harlot by their own deeds. Therefore the wrath of the LORD was kindled against His people, so that He abhorred His own inheritance.

In this psalm shedding "innocent blood" referred to the sacrifice of babies on pagan altars. The book of 2 Kings confirms that infant sacrifice was the key reason that Judah endured drought, famine, plagues, and finally the sword and captivity:

Manasseh shed very much innocent blood, till he had filled Jerusalem from one end to another, besides his sin by which he made Judah sin, in doing evil in the sight of the LORD. (2 Kings 21:16)

Surely at the commandment of the LORD this came upon Judah, to remove them from His sight because of the sins of Manasseh, according to all that he had done, and also because of the innocent blood that he had shed; for he had filled Jerusalem with innocent blood, which the LORD would not pardon. (2 Kings 24:3–4)

"For the children of Judah have done evil in My sight," says the LORD. "They have set their abominations in the house which is called by My name, to pollute it. And they have built the high places of Tophet, which is the Valley of the Son of Hinnom, to burn their sons and their daughters in the fire, which I did not command, nor did it come into My heart. (Jeremiah 7:30–31)

In this light, the anger of heaven must burn against America. The blood of thirty-five million babies cries out to God for vengeance. The blood of thirty-five million babies has been shed, offered to the idol of selfishness on the altar of "choice" in the temples of America's abortion mills.

"But wait!" some will say. "The Bible talks of killing born children. Abortion kills *un*born children." In the eyes of God, there is no difference. God says:

Before I formed you in the womb I knew you; before you were born I sanctified you; I ordained you a prophet to the nations. (Jeremiah 1:5)

For You formed my inward parts; You covered me in my mother's womb. I will praise You, for I am fearfully and wonderfully made; marvelous are Your works, and that my soul knows very well. My frame was not hidden from you, when I was made in secret, and skillfully wrought in the lowest parts of the earth. Your eyes saw my substance, being yet unformed. And in Your book they all were written, the days fashioned for me, when as yet there were none of them. (Psalm 139:13–16)

God miraculously weaves babies together in their mother's womb. Furthermore, God uses the same words (in Greek and Hebrew) to describe a born or a preborn baby. In His mind, both are made in His image, deserving full protection. To snuff out their lives prematurely is murder.

Whether or not we agree with God is irrelevant in this matter. He will render His judgment based on His Laws, not ours. The blood of thirty-five million innocent children must create a deafening howl in the heavens. Because of it, we are in great danger as a nation. Ezekiel recorded these words:

Thus says the LORD God: "The city sheds blood in her own midst, that her time may come; and she makes idols within herself to defile herself. You have become guilty by the blood which you have shed, and have defiled yourself with the idols which you have made. You have caused your days to draw near, and have come to the end of your years; therefore I have made you a reproach to the nations, and a mockery to all countries." (Ezekiel 22:1–4)

HOMOSEXUALITY AND SEXUAL PERVERSIONS

We have become a sex-crazed society. Perversion is rampant; children are molested and abducted; pornography degrades women and men and destroys men, women and children; women are viewed as sex-toys to be used and discarded by vile, pathetic males (I shall not call them men); families are destroyed as a father vents his mid-life crisis by abandoning his wife for a "younger, prettier model"; homosexuals and lesbians are no longer content to secretly live in sin, but now want to glorify their perversions, recruit teenagers to join them, and have everyone accept their vile practices as normal.

The so-called "civil libertarians," who are really cultural barbarians, have declared that pornography is a "right." The American Civil Liberties Union (ACLU) even argued before the Supreme Court *that owning child-pornography is a constitutional right!* Let me state it clearly: pornography is from the pit of hell. Our first amendment was never intended to be abused and twisted so that men, women, and children could be violated and abused like so much meat over the counter.

We are a nation out of control sexually, and our lack of morality is bringing a curse on us.

Now, let me state clearly, God created human sexuality. Sex was God's idea, not man's. But He created it as a beautiful, joyous, private matter to be enjoyed without guilt in the confines of marriage. His Word abounds with clear directives:

> Therefore a man shall leave his father and mother and be joined to his wife, and they shall become one flesh. (Genesis 2:24)

> Drink water from your own cistern, and running water from your own well. Should your fountains

be dispersed abroad, streams of water in the streets? Let them be only your own, and not for strangers with you. Let your fountain be blessed, and rejoice with the wife of your youth. As a loving deer and a graceful doe, let her breasts satisfy you at all times; and always be enraptured with her love. For why should you, my son, be enraptured by an immoral woman, and be embraced in the arms of a seductress? (Proverbs 5:15–20)

The book of the Song of Solomon is a beautiful love poem, dealing with courtship and marriage, and marital love. God is not afraid of or embarrassed by marital relations; He designed them. But He put clear parameters on human sexuality: virginity before marriage, fidelity after marriage.

Many will mock and scoff, but how many "sexually active" young men and young women walk down the marriage aisle are glad *not* to be virgins? Is there a bride who is glad she had other lovers before her husband, or a groom who is glad he had other lovers before his wife? They both wish they did not have the hurts and the memories of other failed relationships. On the other hand, God's design for human sexuality is incredibly liberating, and joyous, and guilt-free.

But many vocal deceivers fancy themselves wiser than God. They believe humans are sexual animals, who jump from bed to bed, fornication to fornication, adulterous relationship to adulterous relationship, and homosexual partner to homosexual partner. These false prophets of sexuality promote the unraveling of our society, and these practices are bringing the judgment of God on our nation.

God has warned us:

"Moreover you shall not lie carnally with your neighbor's wife, to defile yourself with her. And you shall not let any of your descendants pass through the fire to Molech, not shall you profane the name of your God: I *am* the LORD. You shall not lie with male as with a woman. It *is* an abomination. Nor shall you mate with any beast, to defile yourself with it. Nor shall any woman stand before a beast to mate with it. It *is* perversion. Do not defile yourselves with any of these things; for by all these the nations are defiled, which I am casting out before you. For the land is defiled; therefore I visit the punishment of its iniquity upon it, and the land vomits out its inhabitants. You shall therefore keep My statutes and My judgments, and shall not commit *any* of these abominations, *either* any of your own nation or any stranger who sojourns among you. (for all these abominations the men of the land have done, who *were* before you, and thus the land is defiled), lest the land vomit you out also when you defile it, as it vomited out the nations that *were* before you. (Leviticus 18:20–28)

The seven nations that preceded the Israelites were destroyed largely because they had become a sexually perverse society. We know that Sodom and Gomorah were given over to homosexual perversion. And God brought fierce calamity on them.

And the LORD said, "Because the outcry against Sodom and Gomorrah is great, and because their sin is very grave, I will go down now and see whether they have done altogether according to the outcry against it that has come to Me; and if not, I will know." (Genesis 18:20–21)

Now the two angels came to Sodom in the evening, and Lot was sitting in the gate of Sodom. When Lot saw *them*, he rose to meet them, and he bowed himself with his face toward the ground. And he said, "Here now, my lords, please turn in to your servant's house and spend the night, and wash your feet; then you may rise early and go on your way." And they said, "No, but we will spend the night in the open square." But he insisted strongly; so they turned into him and entered his house. Then he made them a feast, and baked unleavened bread, and they ate. Now before they lay down, the men of the city, the men of Sodom, both old and young, all the people from every quarter, surrounded the house. And they called to Lot and said to him, "Where are the men who came to you tonight? Bring them out to us that we may know them *carnally.*" (Genesis 19:1–5)

Then the men said to Lot, "Have you anyone else here? Son-in-law, your sons, your daughters, and whomever you have in the city—take *them* out of this place! For we will destroy this place, because the outcry against them has grown great before the face of the LORD, and the LORD has sent us to destroy it." (Genesis 19:12–13)

Then the LORD rained brimstone and fire on Sodom and Gomorrah, from the LORD out of the heavens. So He overthrew those cities, all the plain, all the inhabitants of the cities, and what grew on the ground (Genesis 19:24-25)

Saint Paul declared:

Likewise also the men, leaving the natural use of the woman, burned in their lust for one another, men with men committing what is shameful, and receiving in themselves the penalty of their error which was due. And even as they did not like to retain God in their knowledge, God gave them over to a debased mind, to do those things which are not fitting; being filled with all unrighteousness, sexual immorality, wickedness, covetousness, maliciousness; full of envy, murder, strife, deceit, evilmindedness; they are whisperers, backbiters, haters of God, violent, proud, boasters, inventors of evil things, disobedient to parents, undiscerning, untrustworthy, unloving, unforgiving, unmerciful; who, knowing the righteous judgment of God, that those who practice such things are deserving of death, not only do the same but also approve of those who practice them. (Romans 1:27–32)

Homosexuality is such a grievous offense, so destructive to society, that God pronounced the death sentence in the Old Testament on those who practiced this abomination.

If a man lies with a male as he lies with a woman, both of them have committed an abomination. They shall surely be put to death. Their blood *shall be* upon them. (Leviticus 20:13)

We may think this is severe, and it is. But this should make us see how dangerous the homosexual rights movement is to the survival of our nation. What horrors await us?

The New Testament offers hope of deliverance and forgiveness to the homosexual through the Lord Jesus Christ.

Do you not know that the unrighteous will not inherit the kingdom of God? Do not be deceived. Neither fornicators, nor idolaters, nor adulterers, nor homosexuals, nor sodomites, nor thieves, nor covetous, nor drunkards, nor revilers, nor extortioners will inherit the kingdom of God. And such were some of you. But you were washed, but you were sanctified, but you were justified in the name of the Lord Jesus and by the Spirit of our God. (1 Corinthians 6:9–11)

In the ranks of the redeemed are sinners of every ilk, men and women who were set free from the vilest of iniquities. God is able to cleanse and forgive. But He is never able to put His stamp of approval on that which He calls an abomination.

The newest homosexual lie is "They do not choose to live this way. They were *born* this way. Who would choose a lifestyle that will bring them ridicule, a lifestyle that may turn their family against them, that may cost them their job; a lifestyle in which they might contract A.I.D.S. and die. Who would *choose* this this? They were born that way!"

At first glance, this may appear like a reasonable argument, but it is not.

For example, a man who commits adultery and leaves his wife and children runs all the same risks. Was he born an adulterer?

A man who is a thief runs all the same risks—except A.I.D.S. (although he may contract A.I.D.S. or tuberculous in prison). Was he born a thief?

A man who molests children—a pedophile—could make all the same arguments. Was he born a pedophile? Should we open our homes to the pedophile? Should we reduce the age of "consensual sex" to twelve years old—

as many have advocated, (including Supreme Court Justice Ruth Ginsburg.) Or should we eliminate any age barrier for sex? Should we "tolerate" the pedophile, "understand" the pedophile, "stop discriminating" against the pedophile because he was "born that way"?

This is the simple truth: God has not called us to tolerate that which he has called an abomination, whether child-killing, pedophilia, or homosexuality. If we do tolerate it and try to normalize it, we simply bring the curse of God on our heads and put our nation on the path of destruction. And no matter what excuses we make, God will honor His Word and will judge the nation that embraces and glorifies perversion.

BLASPHEMY

The Third Commandment says:

> You shall not take the name of the LORD your God in vain, for the LORD will not hold him guiltless who takes His name in vain. (Exodus 20:7)

Yet, the Congress and the President give our hard-earned tax dollars to the National Endowment for the Arts, which then pays "artists" to depict a crucifix floating in a vat of urine or a picture of Christ in His passion with a heroin needle in His arm.

Are we so foolish to think these blasphemies will go unpunished? Malachi warned the Israelites:

> You have wearied the LORD with your words; yet you say, "In what way have we wearied Him?" In that you say, "Everyone who does evil is good in the sight of the LORD, and He delights in them." Or, "Where is the God of justice?" (Malachi 2:17)

When Hollywood produces a film, *The Last Tempta-tion of Christ* which blasphemes the Lord Jesus, do we really think God will turn a blind eye to such insolence?

OTHER SUNDRY SINS

Consider how witchcraft is coming in vogue, even welcomed as another form of spirituality. See how the homosexuals teach their agendas in schools with books like *Heather Has Two Mommies,* and *Daddy's Roommate.* Look at M.T.V. Remember that your tax money funded the "art" of a man urinating in another man's mouth, and a bull-whip inserted in a man's anus.

Look at the messianic state we have created—the state as our healer, our provider, our deliver, our parent, our caretaker in old age. Who needs God?—we have Uncle Sam! How long will God tolerate our false gods that usurp His authority?

Read God's Word about wicked nations, and see why judgment is coming on our nation:

> "For among My people are found wicked men; they lie in wait as one who sets snares; they set a trap; they catch men. As a cage is full of birds, so their houses are full of deceit. Therefore they have be-come great and grown rich. They have grown fat, they are sleek; yes, they surpass the deeds of the wicked; they do not plead the cause, the cause of the fatherless; yet they prosper, and the right of the needy they do not defend. Shall I not punish them for these things?" says the LORD. "Shall I not avenge Myself on such a nation as this?" (Jeremiah 5:26–29)

> Alas, sinful nation, a people laden with iniquity, a brood of evildoers, children who are corrupters! They have forsaken the LORD, they have provoked

to anger the Holy One of Israel, they have turned away backward. (Isaiah 1:4)

They have also built the high places of Baal, to burn their sons with fire for burnt offerings to Baal, which I did not command or speak, nor did it come into My mind. (Jeremiah 19:5)

"Behold, you trust in lying words that cannot profit. Will you steal, murder, commit adultery, swear falsely, burn incense to Baal, and walk after other gods whom you do not know, and then come and stand before Me in this house which is called by My name, and say, 'We are delivered to do all these abominations'? Has this house, which is called by My name, become a den of thieves in your eyes? Behold, I, even I, have seen it," says the LORD. "But go now to My place which was in Shiloh, where I set My name at the first, and see what I did to it because of the wickedness of My people Israel. And now, because you have done all these works," says the LORD, "and I spoke to you, rising up early and speaking, but you did not hear, and I called you, but you did not answer, therefore I will do to the house which is called by My name, in which you trust, and to this place which I gave to you and your fathers, as I have to Shiloh." (Jeremiah 7:8–14)

(In case you are wondering, God destroyed Shiloh.)

It is useless for us to say that God will never judge us, that all Americans are good people, or that our country is a good nation.

Read this warning:

"And I will come near you for judgment; I will be a swift witness against sorcerers, against adulterers, against perjurers, against those who exploit wage earners and widows and orphans, and against those who turn away an alien—because they do not fear Me," say the LORD of hosts. (Malachi 3:5)

Woe to those who rise early in the morning, that they may follow intoxicating drink; who continue until night, till wine inflames them! The harp and the strings, the tambourine and flute, and wine are in their feasts; but they do not regard the work of the LORD, nor consider the operation of His hands. Therefore my people have gone into captivity, because they have no knowledge; their honorable men are famished, and their multitude dried up with thirst. Therefore Sheol has enlarged itself and opened its mouth beyond measure; their glory and their multitude and their pomp, and he who is jubilant, shall descend into it. People shall be brought down, each man shall be humbled, and the eyes of the lofty shall be humbled. But the LORD of hosts shall be exalted in judgment. And God who is holy shall be hallowed in righteousness. Then the lambs shall feed in their pasture, and in the waste places of the fat ones strangers shall eat. Woe to those who draw iniquity with cords of vanity, and sin as if with a cart rope; that say, "Let Him make speed and hasten His work, that we may see it; and let the counsel of the Holy One of Israel draw near and come, that we may know it." Woe to those who call evil good, and good evil; who put darkness for light, and light for darkness; who put bitter for sweet, and sweet for bitter! Woe to those who are wise is their own eyes, and prudent in their own sight! Woe to men mighty at drinking wine, woe to men valiant for mixing intoxicating drink, who justify the wicked for a bribe, and take away justice from the righteous man! Therefore, as the fire devours the stubble, and the flame consumes the chaff, so their root will be as rottenness, and their blossom will ascend like dust; because they have rejected the Law of the LORD of hosts, and despised the word of the Holy One of Israel. Therefore the anger of the LORD is aroused against His people; He has stretched out His hand against them and stricken them, and the hills trembled. Their carcasses *were* as refuse in the midst of the streets. For all this His anger is not turned away, but His hand is stretched out still. (Isaiah 5:11–25)

This reveling, this love of pleasure and drunkenness, this mockery of God, "Let Him make speed and hasten His work, so we may see . . ." describes America perfectly. We are wise in our own eyes, we call the evils of abortion and homosexuality "good," and we vilify the people who fight to protect pre-born children and stand against homosexuals. We glorify the whores and whoremongers of Hollywood and rock and roll, and mock those who proclaim "family values." We have rejected the Law of the Lord, and we are ripe for judgment.

I close this chapter with these verses:

How the faithful city has become a harlot! It was full of justice; righteousness lodged in it, but now murderers. Your silver has become dross, your wine mixed with water. Your princes are rebellious, and companions of thieves; everyone loves bribes, and follows after rewards. They do not defend the fatherless, nor does the cause of the widow come before them. Therefore the LORD says, the LORD of hosts, the Mighty One of Israel, "Ah, I will rid Myself of My adversaries, and take vengeance on My enemies. I will turn My hand against you, and thoroughly purge away your dross, and take away all your alloy. I will restore your judges as at the first, and your counselors as at the beginning. Afterward you shall be called the city of righteousness, the faithful city." (Isaiah 1:21–26)

This last verse provides us with hope and shows us the end that God has in mind: Restoration. In the midst of judgment, may we give God a reason to show mercy and to restore us.

8

WHAT ABOUT THE "INNOCENT"?

For all have sinned and fall short of the glory of God.

Romans 3:22

ONE OF THE MOST VEXING QUESTIONS about judgment is this: "What about the innocent?" What about the Christians who lost their home in the Mississippi River flooding? Or the good people who lost everything in Florida hurricanes? What about 50 percent of the hemophiliacs who have contracted A.I.D.S. because of those homosexuals who have callously polluted the nation's blood supply? What about Kimberly Bergalis—a virgin—who contracted A.I.D.S. from a homosexual dentist?

These heart-wrenching scenarios reveal the deadly nature of sin and judgment. The simple truth is that sin can bring judgment, and judgment can impact non-participants in the sin that brought judgment. More simply put, wickedness hurts the innocent.

If a husband and father commits adultery and abandons his spouse and children, the wife may be destitute, and the children will be fatherless. His children may grow up in severe poverty; they may grow up "dysfunctional"; some of them may even end up in prison. In short, *the children suffer because of the sin of the father.* The children did not do anything wrong, and yet they are in need. The children are innocent of adultery, but they feel the impact and sorrow of the wages of sin. The innocent suffer.

This scenario reveals an aspect of the "covenantal" nature of God and judgment. In other words, it shows that when the covenantal head(s) breaks covenant with God, and God chastens him (or them), those under his care may suffer as well.

When God destroyed Sodom and Gomorah (Genesis 19) by fire and brimstone, because of their wickedness— including vulgar homosexual practices—little children were undoubtedly destroyed in the fire. God judged the heads of houses—as well as the whole house. (see also Joshua 7:20–26)

When Korah and Dathan sinned against the Lord, the ground opened up and swallowed them alive—and their households.

> Now it came to pass, as he finished speaking all these words, that the ground split apart under them, and the earth opened its mouth and swallowed them up, with their households and all the men with Korah, with all their goods. (Numbers 16:31–32)

When the Philistine kings acted wickedly before the Lord by putting the ark of the covenant into the idolatrous temple of the pagan god Dagan, God not only struck them with tumors, He struck the whole nation with tumors (see 1 Samuel 5, especially verse 6).

When Aaron the high priest made a golden calf and led the people in sin, three thousand people died in the judgment of God (see Exodus 32, especially verses 28–31).

These accounts show the critical nature of righteous leadership in the family, church, and government. They should be a sober warning to those—both male and female—who have positions of authority of any kind. May God help us. May He forgive us when we sin and keep those under our care from harm.

I would be amiss if I did not point out another basis for the "innocent" suffering. Simply this: none of us are as "innocent" as we would like to believe. We all (at least all we adults) share in the guilt of this country's moral demise. We all have blood on our hands. Let me explain.

In Leviticus 20:1–5 we read:

> Then the LORD spoke to Moses, saying, "Again, you shall say to the children of Israel: 'Whoever of the children of Israel, who gives any of his descendants to Molech, he shall surely be put to death. The people of the land shall stone him with stones. I will set My face against that man, and will cut him off from his people, because he has given some of his descendants to Molech, to defile My sanctuary and profane My holy name. And if the people of the land should in any way hide their eyes from the man, when he gives some of his descendants to Molech, and they do not kill him, then I will set My face against that man and against his family; and I will cut him off from his people, and all who prostitute themselves with him to commit harlotry with Molech.'"

We see that not only those who kill their children, but also *those who stand by and do nothing are in danger of the judgment of God.*

In Isaiah 1:15–17 we read:

> When you spread out your hands, I will hide My eyes from you; even though you make many prayers, I will not hear. Your hands are full of blood. Wash yourselves, make yourselves clean; put away the evil of your doings from before My eyes. Cease to do evil, learn to do good; seek justice, rebuke the oppressor; defend the fatherless, plead for the widow.

The people praying to God had blood on their hands because they were not rebuking the ruthless, they were not defending the fatherless, they were not protecting the widow. Perhaps they were praying, and were bringing their sacrifices and celebrating the festivals and ceremonies God had appointed. In other words, they were "saved" and went to church regularly, even Wednesday night prayer meeting. And yet God was angry with them and brought judgment on them because they were not exercising righteousness and justice for the oppressed.

This is a perfect reflection of the church today.

We pack out "faith" conferences. We have our religious lingo down pat. But we have sat by idly while millions of babies have been murdered by abortion; we've stood by silently while homosexuals forced their agenda down society's throat; the church and Christian managers (I shrink from calling them leaders) have watched callously while pro-lifers have been beaten by police, sexually molested by prison guards, or sentenced to months or years in jail.

The church in America in many quarters has become little more than a self-help bless-me club. We know little or nothing of sacrifice, of passion for righteousness, of courage in the face of evil. We are the salt that is " . . . good for nothing but to be thrown out and trampled underfoot by men" (Matthew 5:13).

Our laziness, *our* selfishness, and *our* cowardice are all key to America's demise! America could never have become so corrupt so quickly without the complicity of the church. And so judgment will begin with the house of God (1 Peter 4:17).

Ezekiel had a gripping vision which illustrates why passionless believers deserve to share in the judgment:

> And the LORD said to him, "Go through the midst of the city, through the midst of Jerusalem, and put a mark on the foreheads of the men who sigh and cry over all the abominations that are done within it." To the others He said in my hearing, "Go after him through the city and kill, do not let your eye spare, nor have any pity. Utterly slay old and young men, maidens and little children and women; but do not come near anyone on whom is the mark; and begin at My sanctuary." So they began with the elders who were before the temple. Then He said to them, "Defile the temple, and fill the courts with the slain. Go out!" And they went out and killed in the city. So it was that while they were killing them, I was left alone; and I fell on my face and cried out, and said, "Ah, Lord God! Will You destroy all the remnant of Israel in pouring out Your fury on Jerusalem?" Then He said to me, "The iniquity of the house of Israel and Judah *is* exceedingly great, and the land is full of bloodshed, and the city full of perversity; for they say, 'The LORD has forsaken the land, and the LORD does not see!' And as for Me also, My eye will neither spare, nor will I have pity, *but* I will recompense their deeds on their own head." (Ezekiel 9:4–10)

The Lord starts with the elders—church leaders—who are not sighing and crying for the abominations they see. So many Christians and Christian leaders live as if America is not on the brink of destruction. It is "business as usual" for them. God says, "Woe to you who are at ease in Zion..." (Amos 6:1).

If we are at ease, self-absorbed, calloused, cowardly, uninvolved Christians, if we have not rebuked the ruthless and protected the fatherless, then we are also ripe for the judgment of God.

But there is hope. When the full fury of God is poured out in coming years, we have hope from the Scriptures that we can be preserved if we do certain things. The Bible says:

> Seek the LORD, all you meek of the earth, who have upheld His justice. Seek righteousness, seek humility. It may be that you will be hidden in the day of the LORD's anger. (Zephaniah 2:3)

> Then those who feared the LORD spoke to one another, and the LORD listened and heard *them*; so a book of remembrance was written before Him for those who fear the LORD and who meditate on His name. "They shall be Mine," says the LORD of hosts, "On the day that I make them My jewels. And I will spare them as a man spares his own son who serves him." Then you shall again discern between the righteous and the wicked, between one who serves God and one who does not serve Him. (Malachi 3:16–18)

Even though Daniel, Shadrach, Meshach, and Abed-Nego shared in the judgment by being taken as captives to Babylon, God prospered them there and they became key leaders for the whole nation.

So we must not despair! In chapter 10 "The Survival of the Penitent" I will examine what an individual, church, community, and nation can do to avert or deflect the judgment of God.

9

DOES GOD JUDGE NATIONS?

Oh, let the nations be glad and sing for joy! For You shall judge the people righteously, and govern the nations on earth.

S OME WILL NOTICE—EVEN *COMPLAIN*—that most of the warnings of judgment quoted from the Bible are those against the ancient nation of Israel.

That is correct. Those who deride this practice generally build on three theological presumptions.

First, God does not judge heathen nations the way He judged Israel. Second, the standard by which He judged Israel is different from the standard He uses to judge other nations. ("They aren't Christians. They can't be expected to obey God's Law.") Third, God doesn't judge nations in the post-resurrection world; He only judges individuals.

67

I wish to address these lines of reasoning and show that the threatenings of judgment found throughout the Bible have direct bearing on us.

GOD JUDGES HEATHEN NATIONS

First of all, let us see the threats that God's prophets made against heathen (or "non-covenant") nations during the time of Israel. Jeremiah 48 concerns Moab. Here are portions:

Judgment against riches:

Flee, save your lives! And be like the juniper in the wilderness. For because you have trusted in your works and your treasures, you also shall be taken. And Chemosh shall go forth into captivity, his priests and his princes together. And the plunderer shall come against every city; no one shall escape. The valley also shall perish, and the plain shall be destroyed, as the LORD has spoken. Give wings to Moab, that she may flee and get away; for her cities shall be desolate, without any to dwell in them. (vv. 6–9)

Judgment on food supply:

Joy and gladness are taken from the plentiful field and from the land of Moab; I have caused wine to fail from the winepresses; no one will tread with joyous shouting—not joyous shouting! (v. 33)

Drought:

From the cry of Heshbon to Elealeh and to Jahaz they have uttered their voice, from Zoar to Horonaim, like a three-year-old heifer; for the waters of Nimrim also shall be desolate (v. 34).

Sword:

For thus says the LORD: "Behold, one shall fly like an eagle, and spread his wings over Moab. Kerioth is taken, and the strongholds are surprised; the mighty men's hearts in Moab on that day shall be like the heart of a woman in birth pangs." (vv. 40–41)

Why did all this happen?

And Moab shall be destroyed as a people, because he exalted *himself* against the LORD. (v. 42)

"Moreover," says the LORD, "I will cause to cease in Moab the one who offers *sacrifices* in the high places and burns incense to his gods." (v. 35)

But even after these terrifying promises of judgment, God promised restoration:

"Yet I will bring back the captives of Moab in the latter days," says the LORD (v. 47)

In Jeremiah Chapter 50 are prophesies against Babylon. These threatenings mirror the threatenings made against Israel.

"A sword is against the Chaldeans," says the LORD, "Against the inhabitants of Babylon, and against her princes and her wise men. A sword *is* against the soothsayers, and they will be fools. A sword is against her mighty men, and they will be dismayed. A sword is against their horses, against their chariots, and against all the mixed peoples who are in her midst; and they will become like women. A sword is against her treasures, and they will be robbed. A drought is against her waters, and they will be dried up. For it is the land of carved images, and they are insane with their idols. Therefore the wild desert beasts shall dwell there with the jackals, and the ostriches shall dwell in it. It shall be inhabited no more forever, nor shall it be dwelt in from generation to generation. As God overthrew Sodom and Gomorrah and their neighbors," says the LORD, "So no one shall reside there, nor son of man dwell in it." (vv. 35–40)

God said that He would "avenge Himself on His adversaries . . ." in Egypt (Jeremiah 46:10). God announced judgments against the Philistines: "The fathers will not look back for their children, lacking courage" (Jeremiah 47:3), and that He would cause to be heard the "alarm of war." Philistia was to be a "desolate mound" and "her villages shall be burned with fire" (Jeremiah 49:2). Against Kedar He said, "I will bring their calamity from all its sides." (Jeremiah 49:32). And it goes on and on. Lest anyone think proclaimed destruction is limited to Jeremiah, read Isaiah, Ezekiel, Amos, Obadiah, Exodus, Numbers, Joshua, and Jonah.

We see from these passages that God dealt with and judged "heathen" nations in the same way He dealt with Israel.

Also the Scriptures say:

O LORD God, to whom vengeance belongs—O God, to whom vengeance belongs, shine forth! Rise up, O Judge of the earth; render punishment to the proud, LORD, how long will the wicked, how long will the wicked triumph? They utter speech, *and* speak insolent things; all the workers of iniquity boast in themselves. They break in pieces Your people, O LORD, and afflict Your heritage. They slay the widow and the stranger, and murder the fatherless. Yet they say, "The LORD does not see, nor does the God of Jacob understand." Understand, you senseless among the people; and *you* fools, when will you be wise? He who planted the ear, shall He not hear? He who formed the eye, shall He not see? He who instructs the nations, shall He not correct, He who teaches man knowledge? (Psalm 94:1–10)

The LORD *is* at Your right hand; He shall execute kings in the day of His wrath. He shall judge among the nations, He shall fill the places with dead bodies, He shall execute the heads of many countries. (Psalm 110:5–6)

A DIFFERENT STANDARD?

Some sincere Christians believe God uses a different standard by which to judge heathen nations. My first question is, "What standard?" God only has one standard, one law He gave Moses on Mount Sinai, and one Bible He inspired through holy men of God. If God does not hold all nations accountable to His Ten Commandments, then to what does He hold them accountable?

But we know He judges them by His divine standard.

When Gentiles, who do not have the law, by nature do the things in the law, these, although not having the law, are a law to themselves, who show the work of the law written in their hearts, their conscience also bearing witness, and between themselves *their* thoughts accusing or else excusing *them.* (Romans 2:14–15)

The Bible says:

You have rebuked the nations, You have destroyed the wicked; You have blotted out their name forever and ever. But the LORD shall endure forever; He has prepared His throne for judgment. He shall judge the

71

world in righteousness, and He shall administer judgment for the peoples in uprightness. (Psalm 9:5,7–8)

If He judges the world in righteousness, what is the standard of that righteousness? His Law! (See Psalm 19 and Psalm 119.) And again:

> Say among the nations, "The LORD reigns; the world is firmly established, it shall not be moved; He shall judge the peoples righteously." Let the heavens rejoice and let the earth be glad; let the sea roar, and all its fullness; let the field be joyful, and all that is in it. Then all the trees of the woods will rejoice before the LORD. For He is coming, for He is coming to judge the earth. He shall judge the world with righteousness, and the people with His truth. (Psalm 96:10–13)

> He judges the people with truth. Where is truth found? "' . . . Your word is truth'" (John 17:17).

> Let the rivers clap *their* hands; let the hills be joyful together before the LORD, for He is coming to judge the earth. With righteousness He shall judge the world, and the peoples with equity. (Psalm 98:8–9)

From all these scriptures, we see clearly that God judges "heathen" nations according to the standard of His Word. That includes America.

NOT ONLY WITH INDIVIDUALS

Finally, some Christians believe that since the resurrection of Christ, God no long deals with nations, just individuals. That is an absolutely false, unbiblical presupposition.

Revelation 12:5 shows that Christ is the ruler of the nations:

She bore a male Child who was to rule all nations with a rod of iron. And her Child was caught up to God and His throne.

He is the ruler. He is also the judge.

Now I saw heaven opened, and behold, a white horse. And He who sat on him was called Faithful and True, and in righteousness He judges and makes war. His eyes were like a flame of fire, and on His head were many crowns. He had a name written that no one knew except Himself. He was clothed with a robe dipped in blood, and His name is called The Word of God. And the armies in heaven, clothed in fine linen, white and clean, followed Him on white horses. Now out of His mouth goes a sharp sword, that with it He should strike the nations. And He Himself will rule them with a rod of iron. He himself treads the winepress of the fierceness and wrath of Almighty God. And He has on His robe and on His thigh a name written: KING OF KINGS AND LORD OF LORDS.

Psalm 110, a Psalm about Christ after the resurrection reads thus:

The LORD said to my Lord, "Sit at My right hand, till I make Your enemies Your footstool." The LORD shall send the rod of Your strength out of Zion. Rule in the midst of Your enemies! Your people shall be volunteers in the day of Your power; in the beauties of holiness, from the womb of the morning, you have the dew of Your youth. The LORD has sworn and will not relent, "You are a priest forever according to the order of Melchizedek." The LORD is at Your right hand; He shall execute kings in the day of His wrath. He shall judge among the nations, He shall fill the places with dead bodies, He shall execute the heads of many countries. He shall drink of the brook by the wayside; therefore He shall lift up the head.

Jesus Christ is the Sovereign King of kings, the Lord of lords, and He is Judge of the nations. He will bless those nations that obey Him. He will judge those nations that defy Him.

Do we want to know what God will do in the future? We need only look to the past. His laws are unchanging for He is unchanging. We know what kinds of judgment to expect because we see what He did to nations in the past. The threatenings in Deuteronomy 28, Leviticus 26, Amos 4, and all the prophetic books are not just threats against ancient Israel, Babylon, Moab, etc. These threats stand as a warning throughout all time as to how God will deal with the nations who rebel against Him:

> Why do the nations rage, and the people plot a vain thing? The kings of the earth set themselves, and the rulers take counsel together, against the LORD and against His Anointed, saying, "Let us break Their bonds in pieces and cast away Their cords from us."

> He who sits in the heavens shall laugh; the LORD shall hold them in derision. Then He shall speak to them in His wrath, and distress them in His deep displeasure: "Yet I have set My King on My holy hill of Zion."

> "I will declare the decree: the LORD has said to Me, 'You are My Son, today I have begotten You. Ask of Me, and I will give You the nations for Your inheritance. And the ends of the earth for Your possession. You shall break them with a rod of iron; You shall dash them to pieces like a potter's vessel.'"

> Now therefore, be wise, O kings; be instructed you judges of the earth. Serve the LORD with fear, and

rejoice with trembling. Kiss the Son, lest He be angry, and you perish *in* the way, when His wrath is kindled but a little. Blessed *are all those who put their trust in Him.* (Psalm 2)

God judges nations. He uses the standard He has always used—*His righteousness which is outlined in His Law. We do well to remember it.*

PART 4

The Warnings of Judgment

10

BEWARE OF FALSE PROPHETS

They continually say to those who despise Me, "The LORD has said, 'You shall have peace'"; and to everyone who walks according to the dictates of his own heart, they say, "No evil shall come upon you".

Jeremiah 23:17

F ALSE PROPHETS HAVE BEEN A PROBLEM for God since the beginning of time.

When He created Adam and Eve, He made clear that they should not eat of the tree of the knowledge of good and evil, lest they die. (Genesis 2:16–17)

Along comes the first false prophet—a snake—Satan himself, saying "You will not surely die!" (Genesis 3:4). You know the rest of the account. God was telling the truth, the snake was lying, and Adam and Eve charted a course that was to be plagued by false prophets from that day until this.

What was the theme of the snake's lie? "God doesn't mean what He said. If you disobey Him, you won't have any negative repercussions. God won't punish you for your sins. And besides, God is just holding out something good on you!"

And the theme of the false prophets of our day has not changed a bit. *God does not mean what He said. The Ten Commandments aren't for today. God is a God of love: He would never punish you or America for sins committed. Blah, blah, blah.*

It's a disease called hereticulus mouthus diarrheaus. Jeremiah and Ezekiel had to contend with it, as we just read.

While Jeremiah, Ezekiel, and other prophets warned Israel and other nations of the sword that was at their throat, the false prophets undermined their message, gave rebellious sinners false hope and false comfort, and hence actually pushed them toward judgment. A sinner might hear the words of Jeremiah and be overcome with *healthy guilt* (yes, guilt can be healthy)—and the sinner might be on the verge of repenting—when along comes a false prophet saying:

> They continually say to those who despise Me, "The LORD has said, 'You shall have peace'"; and to everyone who walks according to the dictates of his own heart, they say, "No evil shall come upon you". (Jeremiah 23:17)

Now the sinner is numbered and hindered. He feels justified to go on in his sin. "I'm not that bad," he tells himself. "There are a lot of people worse than me. God loves me just as I am."

Who are some of the false prophets of our days?

Non-religious False Prophets

These are the psychiatrists, television and newspaper editors, the college professors, the politicians, the rock and roll stars, the Hollywood psycho-babblers, the high-school guidance counselors, *ad nauseam* who tell their clients, their fans, their followers, and their students, that the Ten Commandments and the Bible are not the infallible Word of God. The Bible is a good book (or a bad book), but it is not the sole, incontestable Word of the Almighty.

For these self-anointed, self-appointed purveyors of wisdom, the thought of God sending people to hell for not believing in and following the Lord Jesus Christ is repugnant. The thought of God sending floods or hurricanes to chasten us is laughable. The thought of God sending A.I.D.S. is outrageous.

If they believe in a god at all, he—or she—is a cosmic new-age marshmallow, or "the force" is everything—the trees, the animals, the water. They have self-consciously rejected the God of the universe.

Well did Paul write of them:

> Although they knew God, they did not glorify Him as God, nor were thankful, but became futile in their thoughts, and their foolish hearts were darkened. Professing to be wise, they became fools, and changed the glory of the incorruptible God into an image made like corruptible man—and birds and four-footed animals and creeping things. Therefore God also gave them up to uncleanness, in the lusts of their hearts, to dishonor their bodies among themselves, who ex- changed the truth of God for the lie, and worshiped and served the creature rather than the Creator, who is blessed forever. (Romans 1:21–25)

These darkened, evil men and women are villains among humanity, evangelists of hell, calloused, brazen souls that are not content to perish in hell forever themselves; they are determined to take others with them. These are destroyers of families, destroyers of daughters, destroyers of sons, who smile and wear nice clothes and use flowery intellectual speech as they subvert righteousness and lead America down a path of destruction.

How can you tell a false prophet? Among other things, he or she will always lead someone away from the Law of God:

> If there arises among you a prophet or a dreamer of dreams, and he gives you a sign or a wonder, and the sign or the wonder comes to pass, of which he spoke to you, saying, "Let us go after other gods"—which you have not known—"and let us serve them," you shall not listen to the words of that prophet or that dreamer of dreams, for the LORD your God is testing you to know whether you love the LORD your God with all your heart and with all your soul. You shall walk after the LORD your God and fear Him, and keep His commandments and obey His voice; you shall serve Him and hold fast to Him." (Deuteronomy 13:1–4)

RELIGIOUS FALSE PROPHETS

Many a man or woman wears a special, "sacred" shawl, reads from a holy book, talks using religious hyperbole, and speaks glowingly of God. However, on close inspection, they do not mean the God of the Bible—the God who gave Ten Commandments to Moses and became man in the Lord Jesus Christ—the only true God. They mean some other god—a far east god or a near east god or a god above or a god below or a whole host of gods. The latter end is the same: they may mean well, they may be sincere, but they are sincerely deceived and sincerely deceiving.

As God has said:

> For you shall worship no other god, for the LORD, whose name is Jealous, is a jealous God. (Exodus 34:14)

> I, *even* I, *am* the LORD, and besides Me *there is* no savior. (Isaiah 43:11)

> I *am* the LORD, that *is* My name; and My glory I will not give to another, nor My praise to carved images. (Isaiah 42:8)

If a religious figure wearing white or black or blue jeans tells you "we're all going to the top of the mountain, we're just going up different sides," he is simply wrong. As Christ said:

> Most assuredly, I say to you, I am the door of the sheep. All who ever came before Me are thieves and robbers, but the sheep did not hear them. I am the door. If anyone enters by Me, he will be saved, and will go in and out and find pasture. The thief does not come except to steal, and to kill, and to destroy. I have come that they may have life, and that they may have it more abundantly. (John 10:7–10)

Furthermore, if a witch or an "Indian spiritualist" or an earth-worshipper or any other priest or priestess of a pagan deity claims to know why the floods and hurricanes have come ("We have offended mother earth"), simply ignore them. I repeat: *ignore them.*

"Christian" Leaders Who Are Not Christian

Tragically, many men who wear a collar and profess to be Christian are liars and deceivers. These men preach from pulpits across America that the clear commandments of God are not clear, that the sinless Son of God was neither sinless nor divine, that the atoning death of Christ and His bodily resurrection were hyperbole, exaggeration and imagination, that the God who promised to judge wicked nations and men judges no one, and that the God who threatens hell will take all into heaven.

This is horrifying. They have the Bible, but they mock it, twist it, and ignore it.

God says:

> "How can you say, 'We are wise, and the law of the LORD is with us'? Look, the false pen of the scribe certainly works falsehood. The wise men are ashamed, they are dismayed and taken. Behold, they have rejected the word of the LORD; so what wisdom do they have? Therefore I will give their wives to others, and their fields to those who will inherit them; because from the least even to the greatest everyone is given to covetousness; from the prophet even to the priest everyone deals falsely. For they have healed the hurt of the daughter of My people slightly, saying, 'Peace, peace!' when there is no peace. Were they ashamed when they had committed abomination? No! They were not at all ashamed, nor did they know how to blush. Therefore they shall fall among those who fall; in the time of their punishment they shall be cast down," says the LORD. (Jeremiah 8:8–12)

It is not enough for them that they speak lies and insurrection against God, but they dare to do it in the name of God and Christ!

God says:

> Her priests have violated My law and profaned My holy things; they have not distinguished between the holy and unholy, nor have they made known *the difference* between the unclean and clean; and they

have hidden their eyes from My Sabbaths, so that I am profaned among them." (Ezekiel 22:26).

Then I said, "Ah, LORD God! Behold, the prophets say to them, 'You shall not see the sword, nor shall you have famine, but I will give you assured peace in this place.'" And the LORD said to me, "The prophets prophesy lies in My name. I have not sent them, commanded them, nor spoken to them; they prophesy to you a false vision, divination, a worthless thing, and the deceit of their heart. Therefore thus says the LORD concerning the prophets who prophesy in My name, whom I did not send, and who say, 'Sword and famine shall not be in this land'—'By sword and famine those prophets shall be consumed! And the people to whom they prophesy shall be cast out in the streets of Jerusalem because of the famine and the sword; they will have no one to bury them—them nor their wives, their sons nor their daughters—for I will pour their wickedness on them.'" (Jeremiah 14:13–16)

These men do more damage than all other false prophets combined, for they lead millions to hell with their lies. They give the unconverted a false hope that they are Christians, even though they reject Christ. They preach in thousands of pulpits—pulpits that once were ablaze with God's truth—that God "understands" and condones abortion, homosexuality, and fornication, that the Ten Commandments were for another time.

These men are wolves in sheep's clothing, a brood of vipers, white-washed tombs, filled with all malice and filth and uncleanness. These men are enemies of the gospel, betrayers of the faith, denying the Lord that bought them, clouds without water, whose end is destruction.

CONFUSED CLERGY

The fourth section of religious leaders who are leading people astray—and I write this section in the fear of God—are the clergy who are truly Christian but are not fulfilling their duty to warn the people of God and the nation of the danger we are in.

God says:

> "Woe to the shepherds who destroy and scatter the sheep of My pasture!" says the LORD. Therefore thus says the LORD God of Israel against the shepherds who feed My people: "You have scattered My flock, driven them away, and not attended to them. Behold, I will attend to you for the evil of your doings," says the LORD. "But I will gather the remnant of My flock out of all countries where I have driven them, and bring them back to their folds; and they shall be fruitful and increase. I will set up shepherds over them who will feed them; and they shall fear no more, nor be dismayed, nor shall they be lacking," says the LORD. (Jeremiah 23:1–4)

How were the shepherds destroying the sheep? By not warning them of the lingering danger.

In Jeremiah's day, people were killed or taken into captivity because of the *lack of warning* from the shepherds. That is a terrifyingly sobering thought. The people suffered because the spiritual leaders did not warn them, prepare them, and even protect them from what was to come.

> Thus says the LORD God: "Woe to the foolish prophets, who follow their own spirit and have seen nothing! O Israel, your prophets are like foxes in the deserts. You have not gone up into the gaps to build a wall for the house of Israel to stand in battle on the day of the LORD." (Ezekiel 13:3–5)

Why? Why do men who are true Christians fail in their duty to warn the flock of God and the nation? Why do they fail to stand as watchmen on the walls? Why do they not stand in the gap?

I believe there are several reasons and there may be one key reason: money.

> Because from the least of them even to the greatest of them, everyone is given to covetousness; and from the prophet even to the priest, everyone deals falsely. They have also healed the hurt of My people slightly, saying, "Peace, peace! When there is no peace." (Jeremiah 6:13–14)

Tragically, many Christian leaders and pastors refuse to declare the whole counsel of God, refrain from preaching the cursings as well as the blessing of God, and shy away from announcing the judgments of God because of money.

- They are burdened by a new building program and do not want to lose tithers.

- They do not want to give a sour note that might adversely affect the offering.

- They do not want to anger the "moderates" on the mailing list.

- They do not want the television or radio audience to stop supporting them financially because they have grown too "negative."

- They do not want to get fired from the congregation because they are so close to retirement.

The scenarios are not uncommon.

Some clergy simply run from controversy. Whether from a personal aversion to conflict, fear of a hostile deacon board or an unhealthy love of reputation (where reputations become an idol), many clergy simply refuse to take a stand on the key Biblical "issues" of the hour.

The true man of God—the "prophet" if you will—will speak the whole counsel of God *no matter what the cost.* And know this, these "prophets" will cause controversy. When the apostles arrived in a new village, the merchants howled:

These men, being Jews, exceedingly trouble our city; and they teach customs which are not lawful for us, being Romans, to receive or observe. (Acts 16:20–21)

When God called Jeremiah, he said:

Behold, I have put My words in your mouth. See, I have this day set you over the nations and over the kingdoms, to root out and to pull down, to build and to plant. (Jeremiah 1:9–10)

Overthrowing and destroying peoples comfortable idolatry is not going to win a man of God awards for being "Mr. Nice Guy." The true man of God, who speaks God's whole counsel, will turn people from sin.

But if they had stood in My counsel, and had caused My people to hear My word, then they would have turned them from their evil way and from the evil of their doings. (Jeremiah 23:22)

The true prophet of God is filled with the Spirit, to declare the sins of the nation.

Now hear this, you heads of the house of Jacob and rulers of the house of Israel, who abhor justice and pervert all equity, who build up Zion with bloodshed and Jerusalem with iniquity: her heads judge for a bribe, her priests teach for pay, and her prophets divine for money. Yet they lean on the LORD, and say, "Is not the LORD among us? No harm can come upon us." Therefore because of you Zion shall be plowed like a field, Jerusalem shall become heaps of ruins, and the mountain of the temple like the bare hills of the forest. (Micah 3:9–12)

This type of ministry will produce enemies. This kind of preaching will outrage the smug. This venue of confronting wickedness will definitely rock the boat. And yet this is what God has called His leaders to do.

In Jesus words:

... If they have called the master of the house Beelzebub, how much more will they call those of his household! (Matthew 10:25)

Blessed are you when they revile and persecute you, and say all kinds of evil against you falsely for My sake. Rejoice and be exceedingly glad, for great is your reward in heaven, for so they persecuted the prophets who were before you. (Matthew 5:11–12)

The false prophet looks out for his own gain. He does not challenge the wicked to leave their sin. He does not announce the terrifying judgments of God. He says God has spoken to him when he has not. He does not speak according to the Law and the testimony, but according to the delusions of his own mind. He declares "peace, peace," when there is no peace, and thereby sets people up for horrifying judgment.

Our nation is polluted with false prophets, littered with non-religious and religious heretics alike, who speak lies in the name of God. And people listen!

Meanwhile, the true church is hampered, shackled, and in some communities crippled by men of God who are afraid to speak the truth. Now more than ever we need servants of the Most High who put God's interest ahead of their own—men who will boldly step forward and confront the lies and deceptions of the false prophets.

Then as God has said:

And he who has My word, let him speak My word faithfully. What *is the chaff to the wheat?* (*Jeremiah 23:28*)

PART 5

The Aftermath of Judgment

11

SURVIVAL OF THE PENITENT

The instant I speak concerning a nation and concerning a kingdom, to pluck up, to pull down, and to destroy it, if that nation against whom I have spoken turns from its evil, I will relent of the disaster that I thought to bring upon it. And the instant I speak concerning a nation and concerning a kingdom, to build and to plant it, if it does evil in My sight so that it does not obey My voice, then I will relent concerning the good with which I said I would benefit it. Now therefore, speak to the men of Judah and to the inhabitants of Jerusalem, saying, "Thus says the LORD: 'Behold, I am fashioning a disaster and devising a plan against you. Return now every one from his evil way, and make your ways and your doings good.'"

Jeremiah 18:7–11

WE ONLY HAVE ONE OPTION if we want to survive as a free nation: we must repent. We must return to the Word of God as our guide and our law in our individual lives, in our families, in our business dealings, in the arts, in medicine, in education, in the judiciary, and in politics. America's moral disintegration into wickedness has been just as comprehensive.

We must repent individually, the Body of Christ must repent corporately, and America must repent nationally.

We must find forgiveness in God for our *own* sins. All of us are sinners, and we all need the grace and forgiveness of God to cleanse us of our sins. Where is this grace found? How is this forgiveness obtained? This grace is found exclusively in the Lord Jesus Christ, and forgiveness is obtained solely by repenting of our sin—turning away from our sin—and believing wholeheartedly in the Lord Jesus Christ.

The Bible says:

> For by grace you have been saved through faith, and that not of yourselves; it is the gift of God, not of works, lest anyone should boast. (Ephesians 2:8–9)

> If you confess with your mouth the Lord Jesus and believe in your heart that God has raised Him from the dead, you will be saved. (Romans 10:9)

If you as an individual want to know assuredly that you have been forgiven by God of your sins here on earth and will spend eternity in heaven with Him, then you must believe in and follow the Lord Jesus Christ. You cannot be forgiven simply by being good, and you cannot get to heaven by trying your very best.

Only the shed blood of Christ—His death on the cross—makes us worthy to stand before God.

As Christ said: "I am the way, the truth, and the life. No one comes to the Father except through Me" (John 14:6).

This means that Buddhists, Hindus, Muslims, and Jews (who don't convert to Christ) will spend eternity in the Lake of Fire. Christ said it clearly:

> Most assuredly, I say to you, he who hears My word
> and believes in Him who sent Me has everlasting life,
> and shall not come into judgment, but has passed
> from death into life. (John 5:24)

For those who believe this too harsh, too unkind, too
final, too "unloving," consider the discussion from
Heaven's viewpoint.

We humans are steeped in sin—rebelling against God,
contriving our own devises and ignoring God's commands. If God were to send us all to hell, none could accuse
Him of being unjust.

> There is none righteous, no, not one; there is none
> who understands; there is none who seeks after God.
> They have all turned aside; they have together become
> unprofitable; there is none who does good, no not
> one. (Romans 3:10–12)

And yet in His love, God became a man in the Lord
Jesus Christ, lived a sinless life, and then died on the cross
for our sins. "For the wages of sin is death" (Romans 6:23),
and Christ paid that penalty for us—death. This is the
extreme God has gone to to provide us salvation. This is
how extreme His love is—a love unto death.

And yet we still rebel. We arrogantly say one religion is
as good as the next. We foolishly proclaim that Christianity
is just one major religion, that Jesus Christ was a great
teacher, but there were many other great teachers. And
then we brazenly say that God would be unjust to send us
to hell for such insolence!

PERSONAL SALVATION VERSUS NATIONAL REFORMATION

Every individual does not need to become a Christian
in order for America to be spared the full fury of God,

which is an earthly, temporal judgment. But every individual needs to become a Christian to be spared the eternal wrath of God, which is a timeless, next world judgment. I hold no hope of every person becoming a Christian, because the Bible does not teach that, but I certainly wish that every person would be a follower of the Lord Jesus Christ.

Furthermore, in terms of national reformation and hopes for national forgiveness from God, even if a homosexual or a child-killer or an adulterer does not become a Christian, it will be better for the nation if he repents of his crimes.

The man or woman who is already a Christian, must too repent. We must repent of our selfishness, our laziness, our cowardice, and our unbiblical retreat into our Christian ghettos, all of which have paved the way for America's demise. We must stop bowing to the idol of our reputation; simply, we must cease loving and saving our own lives.

Jesus said:

"If anyone desires to come after Me, let him deny himself, and take up his cross daily, and follow Me." (Luke 9:23)

We must repent of a "so-called" Christianity that has self at the center and return to a gospel that has Christ at the center. And if obedience to Him means we suffer or we are mocked and ridiculed, so be it. Our lives are His, not our own.

Another part of our repentance must be that we throw off the yoke of bondage and repent of being slaves to every form of iniquity. God has called us to be "the pillar and ground of the truth" (see 1 Timothy 3:15).

God has called us to be like Christ, and He came to earth "that He might destroy the works of the devil" (see 1

John 3:8). We too must stop being sissies and fight to destroy the works of the devil.

Christ said, "I will build My church, and the gates of Hades shall not prevail against it" (Matthew 16:18). We must repent of believing that hell is destined to conquer us.

We must repent of having squandered the freedoms our forefathers fought and sometimes died to give us.

We must repent of having allowed the power bases of civilization to fall into the hands of a pagan elite. You will remember that the hospitals, the orphanages, the arts, the judiciary, the press, the universities, and the schools for children were founded by Christians or developed along the lines of Christian ethics.

Why do you think they call it "*Christian* civilization"? We must repent of having abandoned the power bases which are now being used to oppress us and deliberately seek to rebuild these same power bases on the firm foundation of God's Law.

OUR LIVES AS PREY

If America refuses to repent as a nation, if we keep plummeting into moral anarchy and are judged into oblivion, then certainly preserving our own lives and our families lives from desolation should motivate us to beat our breasts and cry out to God for mercy.

God's Word says:

Gather yourselves together, yes, gather together, O undesirable nation, before the decree is issued, before the day passes like chaff, before the LORD's fierce anger comes upon you, before the day of the LORD's anger comes upon you! Seek the LORD, all you meek of the earth, who have upheld His justice. Seek righteousness, seek humility. It may be that you will be hidden in the day of the LORD's anger. (Zephaniah 2:1–3)

"Son of man, when a land sins against Me by persist-
ent unfaithfulness, I will stretch out My hand against
it; I will cut off its supply of bread, send famine on it,
and cut off man and beast from it. Even *if* these three
men, Noah, Daniel, and Job, were in it, they would
deliver *only* themselves by their righteousness," says
the LORD God. (Ezekiel 14:13–14)

Even if we can't save the nation, we should repent and
live in such a way that God will spare us.
Malachi confirms this principle:

Then those who feared the LORD spoke to one another, and the LORD listened and heard *them;* so a
book of remembrance was written before Him for
those who fear the LORD and who meditate on His
name. "They shall be Mine," says the LORD of hosts,
"On the day that I make them My jewels. And I will
spare them as a man spares his own son who serves
him." Then you shall again discern between the righteous and the wicked, between one who serves God
and one who does not serve Him." (Malachi 3:16–18)

Corporate Confession

But before you give up the battle and seek only to "save
yourselves," let us see how we can perhaps avert the full
fury of God.
Let me state clearly: America will be judged. We have
shed too much blood and practiced too many abominations to walk away unscathed. The question is not, "Will
America be judged?" but rather "How severe will America
be judged?" Or put another way, "Will America be judged
unto restoration or unto annihilation?"
The answer to that, in part, lies with us. *Will we give
God a reason to show mercy in the midst of judgment?*

We must have solemn services where we confess our sins and the sins of the nation. We must be like Daniel who confessed the sins of his people, *even the sins in which he did not personally participate.*

> Then I set my face toward the LORD God to make request by prayer and supplications, with fasting, sackcloth, and ashes. And I prayed to the LORD my God, and made confession, and said, "LORD, great and awesome God, who keeps His covenant and mercy with those who love Him, and with those who keep His commandments, we have sinned and committed iniquity, we have done wickedly and rebelled, even by departing from Your precepts and Your judgments. Neither have we heeded Your servants the prophets, who spoke in Your name to our kings and our princes, to our fathers and all the people of the land.

O LORD, righteousness *belongs* to You, but to us shame of face, as *it is* this day—to the men of Judah, to the inhabitants of Jerusalem and all Israel, those near and those far off in all the countries to which You have driven them, because of the unfaithfulness which they have committed against You. O LORD, to us *belongs* shame of face, to our kings, our princes, and our fathers, because we have sinned against You. To the LORD our God *belong* mercy and forgiveness, though we have rebelled against Him.

We have not obeyed the voice of the LORD our God, to walk in His laws, which He set before us by His servants the prophets. Yes, all Israel has transgressed Your law, and has departed so as not to obey Your voice; therefore the curse and the oath written in the Law of Moses the servant of God have been poured out on us, because we have sinned against Him.

And He has confirmed His words, which He spoke against us and against our judges who judged us, by bringing upon us a great disaster; for under the whole heaven such has never been done as what has been done to Jerusalem.

> As *it is* written in the Law of Moses, all this disaster has come upon us; yet we have not made our prayer before the LORD our God, that we might turn from our iniquities and understand Your truth.

> Therefore the LORD has kept the disaster in mind, and brought it upon us; for the LORD our God is righteous in all the works which He does, though we have not obeyed His voice. And now, O LORD our God, who brought Your people out of the land of Egypt with a mighty hand, and made Yourself a name, as it is this day—we have sinned, we have done wickedly!

> O LORD, according to all Your righteousness, I pray, let Your anger and Your fury be turned away from Your city Jerusalem, Your holy mountain; because for our sins, and for the iniquities of our fathers, Jerusalem and Your people are a reproach to all those around us. Now therefore, our God, hear the prayer of Your servant, and his supplications, and for the LORD's sake cause Your face to shine on Your sanctuary, which is desolate.

> O my God, incline Your ear and hear; open Your eyes and see our desolations, and the city which is called by Your name; for we do not present our supplications before You because of our righteous deeds, but because of Your great mercies.

> O LORD, hear! O LORD, forgive! O LORD, listen and act! Do not delay for Your own sake, my God, for Your city and Your people are called by Your name." (Daniel 9:3–19)

This moving penitent prayer was prayed after horrifying judgments had been poured out and Judah had been in captivity for seventy years. His prayer was heard in heaven. We would do well to follow both the form and substance of Daniel's prayer. God heard his prayer, and the restoration of Judah began shortly after that.

God yet calls to us:

> "I will judge you, O house of Israel, every one according to his ways," says the LORD God. "Repent, and turn from all your transgressions, so that iniquity will not be your ruin. Cast away from you all the transgressions which you have committed, and get yourselves a new heart and a new spirit. For why should you die, O house of Israel? For I have no pleasure in the death of one who dies," says the LORD God. "Therefore turn and live!" (Ezekiel 18:30–32)

Our repentance cannot be obscure or merely "spiritual." God calls us to repent in very concrete, practical ways:

> "Thus says the LORD God: 'Enough, O princes of Israel! Remove violence and plundering, execute justice and righteousness, and stop dispossessing My people,' says the LORD God. 'You shall have honest scales, an honest ephah, and an honest bath.'" (Ezekiel 45:9–10)

> Seek good and not evil, that you may live; so the LORDd God of hosts will be with you, as you have spoken. Hate evil, love good; establish justice in the gate. It may be that the LORD God of hosts will be gracious to the remnant of Joseph. (Amos 5:14–15)

> "When you spread out your hands, I will hide My eyes from you; even though you make many prayers, I will

not hear. Your hands are full of blood. Wash your-selves, make yourselves clean; put away the evil of your doings from before My eyes. Cease to do evil, learn to do good; seek justice, rebuke the oppressor; defend the fatherless, plead for the widow. Come now, and let us reason together," says the LORD, "Though your sins are like scarlet, they shall be as white as snow; though they are red like crimson, they shall be as wool. If you are willing and obedient, you shall eat the good of the land; but if you refuse and rebel, you shall be devoured by the sword"; for the mouth of the LORD has spoken. (Isaiah 1:15–20)

Finally, besides individual repentance and church re-pentance, we need some kind of repentance as a nation. That in part means our political leaders must bow their knee before God and admit that they have done wickedly, that we as a nation have acted corruptly.

Even when God was threatening the devastation of Judah, he was offering the kings of Judah a mitigation of the sentence, if they would repent of their iniquities.

Thus says the LORD: "Go down to the house of the king of Judah, and there speak this word, and say, "Hear the word of the LORD, O king of Judah, you who sit on the throne of David, you and your servants and your people who enter these gates! Thus says the LORD: "Execute judgment and righteousness, and de-liver the plundered out of the hand of the oppressor. Do no wrong and do no violence to the stranger, the fatherless, or the widow, nor shed innocent blood in this place. For if you indeed do this thing, then shall enter the gates of this house, riding on horses and in chariots, accompanied by servants and people, kings who sit on the throne of David. But if you will not hear these words, I swear by Myself," says the LORD, "that this house shall become a desolation.'" (Jeremiah 22:1–5)

Judah's kings, however, were arrogant and brazen in their sin. Not only did they not repent, but King Ahaz (and thousands of others) died in captivity, and King Zedekiah had his eyes gouged out after he saw his sons slain before him. They say the cost is high to serve God. The way of sin is far more costly.

Hear the prayer of King Solomon:

And may You hear the supplications of Your servant and of Your people Israel, when they pray toward this place. Hear from heaven Your dwelling place, and when You hear, forgive. If anyone sins against his neighbor, and is forced to take an oath, and comes and takes an oath before Your altar in this temple, then hear from heaven, and act, and judge Your servants, bringing retribution on the wicked by bringing his way on his own head, and justifying the righteous by giving him according to his righteousness. Or if Your people Israel are defeated before an enemy because they have sinned against You, and return and confess Your name, and pray and make supplication before You in this temple, then hear from heaven and forgive the sin of Your people Israel, and bring them back to the land which You gave to them and their fathers. When the heavens are shut up and there is no rain because they have sinned against You, when they pray toward this place and confess Your name, and turn from their sin because You afflict them, then hear in heaven, and forgive the sin of Your servants, Your people Israel, that You may teach them the good way in which they should walk; and send rain on Your land which You have given to Your people as an inheritance. When there is famine in the land, pestilence or blight or mildew, locusts or grasshoppers;

when their enemies besiege them in the land of their cities; whatever plague or whatever sickness there is; whatever prayer, whatever supplication is made by anyone, or by all Your people Israel, when each one knows his own burden and his own grief, and spreads out his hands to this temple: then hear from heaven Your dwelling place, and forgive, and give to everyone according to all his ways, whose heart You know (for You alone know the hearts of sons of men), that they may fear You, to walk in Your ways as long as they live in the land which You gave to our fathers. (2 Chronicles 6:21–31)

When they sin against You (for there is no one who does not sin), and You become angry with them and deliver them to the enemy, and they take them captive to a land far or near; yet when they come to themselves in the land where they were carried captive, and repent, and make supplication to You in the land of their captivity, saying, "We have sinned, we have done wrong, and have committed wickedness"; and when they return to You with all their heart and with all their soul in the land of their captivity, where they have been carried captive, and pray toward their land which You gave to their fathers, the city which You have chosen, and toward the temple which I have built for Your name: then hear from heaven Your dwelling place their prayer and their supplications, and maintain their cause, and forgive Your people who have sinned against You. (2 Chronicles 6:36–39)

If America is going to be spared, we must repent.

- That means that we confess our sins, and *we alter our behavior.*

- It means the owners of M.T.V. repent for glorifying wickedness.

- It means our political leaders repent for subsidizing blasphemy.

- It means our judges will repent (and/or be replaced) for trying to stamp God out of schools, history books, and "public property."

- It means our abortion mills are closed, and child-killing is illegal again.

- It means homosexuals are not given special rights, but homosexuality is again considered what it has been for centuries: wicked, criminal behavior.

- It means tax-payers are not forced to pay for pagan education.

- It means we do not push condoms in our schools.

- It means Hollywood repents of making movies that blaspheme Christ or use His name in vain or glorify adultery and promiscuity.

- It means our government repents of manipulating us, stealing from us, and believing that Uncle Sam is our savior.

- It means we self-consciously seek to live our lives, educate our children, run our businesses, adjudicate in courts of law, and govern our nation *in the fear of God.*

The fear of God is the beginning of wisdom. (Proverbs 1:7)

The fear of God is to hate evil. (Proverbs 8:13)

The fear of the LORD is clean, preserving the soul. (Psalm 19:9)

This nation needs to return to the fear of God. Perhaps then God will allow us to rebuild a free, prosperous nation, one that honors Him and blesses the nations of the earth.

We have a wonderful illustration of national repentance and repentance in political leaders in the book of Jonah:

> Now the word of the LORD came to Jonah the second time, saying, "Arise, go to Nineveh, that great city, and preach to it the message that I tell you." So Jonah arose and went to Nineveh, according to the word of the LORD. Now Nineveh was an exceedingly great city, a three-day journey in extent. And Jonah began to enter the city on the first day's walk. Then he cried out and said, "Yet forty days, and Nineveh shall be overthrown!" So the people of Nineveh believed God, proclaimed a fast, and put on sackcloth, from the greatest to the least of them. Then word came to the king of Nineveh; and he arose from his throne and laid aside his robe, covered himself with sackcloth and sat in ashes. And he caused it to be proclaimed and published throughout Nineveh by the decree of the king and his nobles, saying, "Let neither man nor beast, herd nor flock, taste anything; do not let them eat, or drink water. But let man and beast be covered with sackcloth, and cry mightily to God; yes, let every one turn from his evil way and from the violence that is in his hands. Who can tell if God will turn and relent, and turn away from His fierce anger, so that we may not perish?"

Then God saw their works, that they turned from their evil way; and God relented from the disaster that He had said He would bring upon them, and He did not do it. (Jonah 3)

Would to God that we had civic leaders that recognized the great danger we are in and led the nation in repentance.

It has happened in our nation before. Between 1795 and 1800, we were facing an unwanted war with France, a war we could easily have lost.

President Adams issued the following proclamation:

As the safety and prosperity of nations ultimately and essentially depends on the protection and the blessing of Almighty God, and the national acknowledgment of truth is not only an indispensable duty which the people owe to Him, but a duty whose natural influence is favorable to the promotion of that morality and piety without which social happiness can not exist nor the blessings of a free government be enjoyed; and as this duty, at all times incumbent, is so especially in seasons of difficulty or danger, when existing or threatening calamities, the just judgment of God against prevalent iniquities, are a loud call to repent and reform; and as the United States of America are at present placed in a hazardous and afflictive situation by the unfriendly disposition, conduct, and demands of a foreign power, evidenced by repeated refusals to receive our messengers of reconciliation and peace, by depredations on our commerce, and the infliction of injuries on very many of our fellow-citizens, while engaged on their lawful business on the seas—it has appeared to me that the duty of imploring the mercy and benediction of Heaven on our country demands at this time a special attention from its inhabitants.

I have therefore thought fit to recommend, and I do hereby recommend that Wednesday, the 9th day of May next, be observed throughout the United States as a day of solemn humiliation, fasting, and prayer; that the citizens of these states, abstaining on that day from their customary worldly occupations offer their devout addresses to the Father of Mercies agreeably to those forms and methods which they have severally adopted as the most suitable and becoming; that all religious congregations do, with the deepest humility acknowledge before God the manifold sins and transgressions with which we are justly chargeable as individuals and as a nation, beseeching Him at the same time of His infinite grace, through the Redeemer of the World, freely to remit all our offenses and to incline us by His Holy Spirit to that sincere repentance and reformationwhich may afford us reason to hope for His inestimable favor and heavenly benediction; that it be made the subject of particular and earnest supplication that our country may be protected from all the dangers that threaten it; that our civil and religious privilegesmay be preserved inviolate and perpetuated to the latest generations. . .

And finally I recommend that on the said day, the duties of humiliation and prayer be accompanied by fervent thanksgiving to the Bestower of Every Good Gift, not only for his hitherto having protected and preserved the people of these United States in the independent employment of their religious and civil freedom, but also for having prospered them in a wonderful progress of population, and for conferring on them many and great favors conducive the happiness and prosperity of a nation. Given under my hand and the seal of the United States of America at Philadelphia, this 23rd day of March, A.D. 1798, and of the Independence of the said states, the twenty-second.

May God restore to us—through our hard work and prayers—men of this caliber and stature.

12

Rebuilding Our Nation

Those from among you shall build the old waste places; you shall raise up the foundations of many generations; and you shall be called the Repairer of the Breach, the Restorer of Streets to Dwell in.

Isaiah 58:12

COMING RUBBLE. COMING DISASTER. New leaders will arise. New leaders will be sought. Who will they be? Those who will be the leaders must speak boldly now.

Reclaim the Power Bases and Rebuild the Nation

Disaster is coming. America is going to enter a season of turbulence and turmoil that it has never known: an era of upheaval and convulsion that will dwarf the unrest of the sixties. We are going to tumble into economic and social chaos, a period where the Los Angeles riots could be duplicated in cities across the nation; a living nightmare that could make the civil war look civil. We will be floundering in confusion, surrounded by rubble—both figuratively and literally in many cases.

In that hour, America will clamor for new leaders. In that season, individuals will desperately seek strong and, if need be, authoritarian visionaries to rebuild out of the rubble.

The critical question is this: who will rebuild out of the coming chaos? Who will rebuild out of the rubble?

Will it be righteous men and women who cherish freedom, or iron fisted tyrants?

The prophet Isaiah gave the call, which echoes in our day:

> "The Spirit of the LORD God is upon Me, because the LORD has anointed Me to preach good tidings to the poor; He has sent Me to heal the brokenhearted, to proclaim liberty to the captives, and the opening of the prison to those who are bound; to proclaim the acceptable year of the LORD, and the day of vengeance of our God; to comfort all who mourn, to console those who mourn in Zion, to give them beauty for ashes, the oil of joy for mourning, the garment of praise for the spirit of heaviness; that they may be called trees of righteousness, the planting of the LORD, that He may be glorified." And they shall rebuild the old ruins, they shall raise up the former desolations, and they shall repair the ruined cities, the desolations of many generations. (Isaiah 61:1-4)

God has called His people to be those who rebuild the waste places on the unshakeable foundation of God's Law, those who restore the cities according to Biblical principles.

Will We Be Ready?

But that does not mean we will be ready. And if we are not ready, a worse fate may await us: unbridled tyranny.

One thing is certain: chaos and turmoil produce springboards for new leaders. However, while chaos may result in a George Washington, it may also result in an Adolf Hitler.

In the late 1920s and early 1930s, Germany was in chaos. The nation was humiliated in its defeat in World War 1 and subsequent treaties it was forced to sign. Its people were demoralized. Society was breaking down. Hyperinflation had wiped out the middle class. People had to bring a wheel barrel full of reichsmarks (paper money) to buy a loaf of bread. In the midst of this societal rubble rose a man with vision, a man who seemed unshakable, and a man who inspired hope and confidence: Adolf Hitler.

Adolf Hitler, the demonized, God-hating, murderous villain, could never have risen to such stature had there not been a mound of rubble on which he could stand. The German people would not have been so susceptible to an evil demagogue had they not been desperate for solutions, desperate for a leader or leaders to lead them out of disgrace.

The Scriptures speak of this desperation in times of crisis:

And in that day seven women shall take hold of one man, saying, "We will eat our own food and wear our own apparel; only let us be called by your name, to take away our reproach." (Isaiah 4:1)

When a man takes hold of his brother in the house of his father, saying, "You have clothing; you be our ruler, and let these ruins be under your power," in that day he will protest, saying, "I cannot cure your

111

ills, for in my house is neither food nor clothing; do not make me a ruler of the people." (Isaiah 3:6–7)

These Scriptures also show that humanity can be as foolish as they are desperate when clamoring for a leader. A man's solutions may be from the pit of hell; a man's allegiance may be to paganism; a man's vision may be to build a tyrannical, oppressive regime—but if he is confident, courageous, and exemplifies leadership and vision in the midst of fear and turmoil, people will follow him.

As you can guess, this makes a nation very vulnerable in times of crisis. It makes men more willing to believe lies, more eager to overlook glaring faults and ignore the dark clouds of warning: clouds of warning that clearly spell oppression, slavery, and death to clear thinking individuals.

How do we get good men in position? I will put Christian civilization up against paganism, fascism, hedonism, socialism any day of the week, yet will we have Christian men in position?

The problem is, in the midst of crisis, folks are so desperate for solutions *now*, so anxious to alleviate hardship *now*, that they fail to ask the simple questions: "Where is this taking us? Where is this man, or where are these men and their political philosophy ultimately going to lead us?"

Both Winston Churchill and Adolf Hitler rose quickly to incredible heights of leadership because their nations were in crisis (albeit for very different reasons). Winston Churchill was fighting for freedom. Adolf Hitler was fighting for slavery.

In the midst of our coming national crisis when the public is clamoring for new leaders and solutions, who will emerge to lead? In our most vulnerable hour, when chaos, calamity, and cultural anarchy are standard fare, will we have righteous men and women, champions of freedom (as

God's Word defines freedom) rise up and lead? Or will we be plagued with tyrants in two-piece suits? Will the nation fall prey to a slick-talking leader whose ÒformÓ appeals to us—the form of passion and confidence and courage but whose substance is oppressive, paganistic, barbarism?

Remember both Churchill and Hitler showed incredible courage. Both were inspirational. Both had charismatic personalities. Only the substance of their political ideologies separated them. The source of Hitler's ethics made him demonic, evil, sinister, and vile. And the source of Churchill's ethics made him fight for the preservation of Christian civilization.

So the question facing us in our hour of crisis is, which leader will emerge? Winston Churchills or Adolf Hitlers?

Having the Righteous Ready

The prophet, Jeremiah, provides us a critical principle in determing who will lead us out of disaster. Jeremiah spoke the truth when the truth was unpopular. Jeremiah warned of the coming disaster and judgment and told people what they needed to do to avert disaster and rebuild their country.

Because of Jeremiah's stand for justice and righteousness, he was vilified, despised, and scorned. But ultimately, God showed him that his enemies would clamor for his advice.

> Woe is me, my mother, that you have borne me, a man of strife and a man of contention to the whole earth! I have neither lent for interest, nor have men lent to me for interest. Every one of them curses me. The LORD said: "Surely it will be well with your remnant; surely I will cause the enemy to intercede with you in the time of adversity and in the time of affliction." (Jeremiah 15:10–11)

It was not easy for Jeremiah. He prophesied destruction and ruin when such declarations appeared to be the fanatical babblings of a madman.

> I am in derision daily; everyone mocks me. For when I spoke, I cried out; I shouted, "Violence and plunder!" Because the word of the LORD was made to me a reproach and a derision daily. (Jeremiah 20:7–8)

Part of being a leader is seeing ahead. We must be visionaries. At times that means we see the danger coming, and we warn people of disaster, even if they don't listen. This can be an agonizing experience, as it was for Jeremiah, because it involves feeling the emotions of dread and anguish, only to have people ignore you.

> O my soul, my soul! I am pained in my very heart! My heart makes a noise in me; I cannot hold my peace, because you have heard, O my soul, the sound of the trumpet, the alarm of war. Destruction upon destruction is cried, for the whole land is plundered. Suddenly my tents are plundered, and my curtains in a moment. How long will I see the standard, and hear the sound of the trumpet? "For my people are foolish, they have not known Me. They are silly children, and they have no understanding. They are wise to do evil, but to do good they have no knowledge." (Jeremiah 4:19–22)

What makes this even more difficult for us, is that we may be required to speak out for years without our warnings being heeded and without disaster actually coming.

Imagine this scenario with me. Imagine Jeremiah preaching in front of the Temple in Jerusalem in the first year of his prophetic calling. A thirty-two-year-old dad had taken his twelve-year-old son into the temple, and they pass Jeremiah, who stands prophesying:

> "Behold, he shall come up like clouds, and his chariots like a whirlwind. His horses are swifter than eagles. Woe to us, for we are plundered!" O Jerusalem, wash your heart from wickedness, that you may be saved. How long shall your evil thoughts lodge within you? For a voice declares from Dan and proclaims affliction from Mount Ephraim: "Make mention to the nations, yes, proclaim against Jerusalem, that watchers come from a far country and raise their voice against the cities of Judah. Like keepers of a field they are against her all around, because she has been rebellious against Me," says the LORD. "Your ways and your doings have procured these things for you. This is your wickedness, because it is bitter, because it reaches to your heart." (Jeremiah 4:13–18)

The boy walks by wide-eyed, half frightened, half shocked. Once passed Jeremiah, however, he asks his dad, "Father, is that man telling us the truth? Is God going to punish us?"

The father response is swift, "Son, that man is crazy. We are God's people. We are Israel. No evil will befall us. We have the Temple of the Lord, the very house of God."

The little boy grows up, seeing and hearing Jeremiah from time to time over the years. He marries at age nineteen, and he and his wife have a son. When his son is six years old, he takes him to the Temple for the first time. They pass Jeremiah, who is yet prophesying the judgment of God.

> Therefore you shall say this word to them: "Let my eyes flow with tears night and day, and let them not cease; for the virgin daughter of my people has been

broken with a mighty stroke, with a very severe blow. If I go out to the field, then behold, those slain with the sword! And if I enter the city, then behold, those sick from famine! Yes, both prophet and priest go about in a land they do not know." (Jeremiah 14:17–18)

The man's six-year-old son watches and listens with amazement, and then asks his dad, "Papa, is that man a good man? Is God going to judge us?"

"Son," the father confidently replies, "that man is crazy. He has been saying these things for thirteen years. I heard him when I was a boy with my father. None of his prophesies have happened yet." Then he turns to Jeremiah, "Hey, Jeremiah, why don't you get a new message! That one is not producing too many converts, and none of what you declare has come to pass!"

It had to be demoralizing for Jeremiah. At times he was deeply angry with the people for not listening:

Oh, that my head were waters, and my eyes a fountain of tears, that I might weep day and night for the slain of the daughter of my people! Oh, that I had in the wilderness a lodging place for travelers; that I might leave my people, and go from them! For they are all adulterers, an assembly of treacherous men. (Jeremiah 9:1–2)

O LORD, You know; remember me and visit me, and take vengeance for me on my persecutors. In Your enduring patience, do not take me away. Know that for Your sake I have suffered rebuke. Your words were found, and I ate them, and Your word was to me the joy and rejoicing of my heart; for I am called by Your name, O LORD God of hosts. I did not sit in the assembly of the mockers, nor did I rejoice; I sat alone because of Your hand, for You have filled me with indignation. Why is my pain perpetual and my wound incurable, which refuses to be healed? Will You surely be to me like an unreliable stream, as waters that fail? (Jeremiah 15:15–18)

At times he was angry with God and decided he would stop prophesying!
But he couldn't do it.

Then I said, "I will not make mention of Him, nor speak anymore in His name." But His word was in my heart like a burning fire shut up in my bones; I was weary of holding it back, and I could not. (Jeremiah 20:9)

If righteous men and women want to have credibility on the other side of the coming crisis, they must speak the truth unflinchingly now. We must be willing to say and do what is right, even when it is unpopular, when it is not "politically correct." We must have the courage to proclaim the coming danger, and proclaim solutions now, so that when all hell breaks loose, the nation will look to the righteous to rebuild the country on the Ten Commandments, instead of on more messianic statism sold to us by another pagan politician.

Let me again note recent history. Churchill rose so quickly from the back bench of parliament to become prime minister because he had warned all England of the coming "rain of fire and steel" that Hitler would bring. Throughout the 1930s, he prophesied the coming devastation. He warned them when it was politically unpopular to do so, when the press vilified him as a warmonger and a fearmonger, when fellow members of parliament hissed him and booed him for saying that Germany was a menace and that Hitler was a madman that must be hemmed in and destroyed.

But when the bombs started falling, when Prague fell and Poland fell and the Lowland fell and finally France fell, England looked to him to lead the people through the crisis. He had earned their trust. He had warned them. He didn't have the blood of British soldiers and citizens on His hands.

Of course, there is one other tragic historical footnote. The Allies delivered Eastern Europeans out of the clutches of one tyrant only to deliver them into the hand of another—Joseph Stalin.

I can only hope that the righteous will rise up and rebuild out of our own coming rubble. But frankly, I don't know if we will. Over the past two generations, by and large, the wicked who reject God's Law have shown more courage, passion, and vision in their godless agenda than the righteous who believe in God's Law.

Look at the zeal of the wicked:

> Their feet run to evil, and they make haste to shed innocent blood; their thoughts are thoughts of iniquity; wasting and destruction are in their paths. The way of peace they have not known, and there is no justice in their ways; they have made themselves crooked paths; whoever takes that way shall not know peace. (Isaiah 59:7–8)

Then look at the mediocrity of the righteous:

> We grope for the wall like the blind, and we grope as if we had no eyes; we stumble at the noonday as at twilight; we are as dead men in desolate places. We all growl like bears, and moan sadly like doves; we look for justice, but there is none; for salvation, but it is far from us. (Isaiah 59:10–11)

If this nation is going to be rebuilt into a just and righteous republic, we must begin fighting now. If we don't stand and speak and act unwaveringly now, we will not have the respect and the credibility to lead and serve later.

On the contrary, we may be the scapegoat. Adolf Hitler used the Jews and certain Christians as scapegoats for Germany's troubles. Will a new breed of pagans rise to power and blame America's collapse on "religious extremists, fundamentalists, and the Christian right"? It's possible; don't kid yourself otherwise.

Finally, what if our nation doesn't survive? What if the Union breaks up? What if the United States goes the way of the Union of Soviet Socialist Republics (U.S.S.R.)? It could happen. We could fragment and splinter in any number of directions.

Should that happen, what types of new nations will arise from the ashes of the United States? Will they be God-honoring, free societies? Will they be laboratory studies in socialism? Will we have Patrick Henrys who rise up and say, "Is life so dear, or peace so sweet, as to be purchased at the price of chains and slavery? Forbid it, Almighty God! I know not what course others may take; but as for me, give me liberty, or give me death"(from speech in Virginia in the convention at Richmond, March 23, 1775)?

Will we have Theodore Roosevelts who rise up to lead one of the new nations, saying:

> Progress has brought us both unbounded opportunities and unbridled difficulties. Thus, the measure of our civilization will not be *that* we have done much but *what* we have done with that much. I believe that the next half century will determine if we will advance the cause of Christian civilization or revert to the horros of brutal paganism. The thought of modern

industry in the hands of Christian charity is a dream worth dreaming. The thought of industry in the hands of paganism is a nightmare beyond imagining. The choice between the two is upon us.

There are those who believe that a new modernity demands a new morality. What they fail to consider is the harsh reality that there is no such thing as a new morality. There is only one morality. All else is immorality. There is only true Christian ethics over against which stands the whole of paganism. If we are to fulfill our great destiny as a people, then we must return to the old morality, the sole morality.

We can only pray and hope so. But before we worry about running against heroes, we had better run with footmen.

We must prove our valor, our loyalty, *now*. We must offer God's solutions *now*. We must hold up the flawless, unchanging, unimprovable standard of God's Law *now*— *now* while the pagan elite mock us, *now* while the socialist planners deride us, *now while the millions misunderstand us. If we are faithful at our post, God will honor us, and the nation will look to the righteous, who herald God's righteous principles to rebuild the United States from the coming rubble.*

If not, we and our seed may well perish.

The Death of a Nation

I N ORDER TO ISOLATE THEMES OF JUDGMENT— such as famine or the sword—I have quoted verses from various passages, showing that God has definite stages in judgment. But Scripture paints a cohesive picture of the comprehensive horrifying experience of judgment.

This is not an abstract study in Bible class; we are speaking of plagues that will claim loved ones, floods or drought that could rob us of our life savings, the sword that could cut our sons and daughters.

The specter of this definitive judgment may shock us into repentance and obedience; it may literally scare the hell out of us. We must see for ourselves the individual verses quoted in the context of total terrifying judgment. And so I give you some more Bible passages for your study.

> Then, if you walk contrary to Me, and are not willing to obey Me, I will bring on you seven times more plagues, according to your sins. I will also send wild beasts among you, which shall rob you of your children, destroy your livestock, and make you few in number; and your highways shall be desolate. And if by these things you are not reformed by Me, but walk contrary to Me, then I also will walk contrary to you,

and I will punish you yet seven times for your sins. And I will bring a sword against you that will execute the vengeance of the covenant; when you are gathered together within your cities I will send pestilence among you; and you shall be delivered into the hand of the enemy. When I have cut off your supply of bread, ten women shall bake your bread in one oven, and they shall bring back your bread by weight, and you shall eat and not be satisfied. (Leviticus 26:21–25)

For a fire is kindled in My anger, and shall burn to the lowest hell; it shall consume the earth with her increase, and set on fire the foundations of the mountains. I will heap disaster on them; I will spend My arrows on them. They shall be wasted with hunger, devoured by pestilence and bitter destruction; I will also send against them the teeth of beasts, with the poison of serpents of the dust. The sword shall destroy outside; there shall be terror within for the young man and virgin, the nursing child with the man of gray hair. (Deuteronomy 32:22–25)

But it shall come to pass, if you do not obey the voice of the LORD your God, to observe carefully all His commandments and His statutes which I command you today, that all these curses will come upon you and overtake you: cursed shall you be in the city and cursed shall you be in the country. Cursed shall be your basket and your kneading bowl. Cursed shall be the fruit of your body and produce of your land, the increase of your cattle and the offspring of your flocks. Cursed shall you be when you come in, and cursed shall you be when you go out. The LORD will send on you cursing, confusion, and rebuke in all that you set your hand to do, until you are destroyed and until you perish quickly, because of the wickedness of your doings in which you have forsaken Me. The LORD will make the plague cling to you until He has consumed you from the land which you are going to possess. The LORD will strike you with consumption, with fever, with inflammation, with severe burning fever, with the sword, with scorching, and with mildew; they shall pursue you until you perish. And your heavens which are over your head shall be bronze, and the earth which is under you shall be iron. The LORD will change the rain of your land to powder and dust; from the heaven it shall come down on you until you are destroyed. The LORD will cause you to be defeated before your enemies; you shall go out one way against them and flee seven ways before them; and you shall become troublesome to all the kingdoms of the earth. Your carcasses shall be food for all the birds of the air and beasts of the earth, and no one shall frighten them away. The LORD will strike you with the boils of Egypt, with tumors, with the scab, and with the itch, from which you cannot be healed. The LORD will strike you with madness and blindness and confusion of heart. And you shall grope at noonday, as a blind man gropes in the darkness; you shall not prosper in your ways; you shall be only oppressed and plundered continually, and no one shall save *you*. You shall betroth a wife, but another man shall lie with her; you shall build a house, but you shall not dwell in it; you shall plant a vineyard, but shall not gather its grapes. Your ox shall be slaughtered before your eyes, but you shall not eat of it; your donkey shall be violently taken away from before you, and shall not be restored to you; your sheep shall be given to your enemies, and you shall have no one to rescue them. Your sons and your daughters shall be given to another people, and your eyes shall look and fail with longing for them all day long; and there shall be no strength in your hand. A nation whom you have not known shall eat the fruit of your land and the produce of your labor, and you shall be only oppressed and crushed continually. So you shall be driven mad because of the sight which your eyes see. The LORD will strike you in the knees and on the legs with severe boils which cannot be healed, and from the sole of your foot to the top of your head. The LORD will bring you and the king whom you set over you to a nation which neither you nor your fathers have known, and there you shall serve other gods—wood and stone. And you shall become an astonishment, a proverb, and a byword among all nations where the LORD will drive you. You shall carry much seed out to the field but gather little in, for the locust shall consume it. You shall plant vineyards and tend them, but you shall neither drink of the wine nor gather the grapes; for the worms shall eat them. You shall have olive trees throughout all your territory, but you shall not anoint yourself with the oil; for your olives shall drop off. You shall beget sons and daughters, but they shall not be yours; for they shall go into captivity. Locusts shall consume all your trees and the produce of your land. The alien who is among you shall rise higher and higher above you, and you shall come down lower and lower. He shall lend to you, but you shall not lend to him; he shall be the head, and you shall be the tail. Moreover all these curses shall come upon you and pursue and overtake you, until you are destroyed, because you did not obey the voice of the LORD your God, to keep His commandments and His statutes which He commanded you. And they shall be upon you for a sign and a wonder, and on your descendants forever. Because you did not serve the LORD your God with joy and gladness of heart, for the abundance of everything, therefore you shall serve your enemies, whom the LORD will send against you, in hunger, in thirst, in nakedness, and in need of everything; and He will put a yoke of iron on your neck until He has destroyed you. The LORD will bring a nation against you from afar, from the end of the earth, as swift as the eagle flies, a nation whose language you will not understand, a nation of fierce countenance, which does not respect the elderly nor show favor to the young. And they shall eat the increase of your livestock and the produce of your land, until you are destroyed; they shall not leave you grain or new wine or oil, *or* the increase of your cattle or the offspring of your flocks, until they have destroyed you. They shall besiege you at all your gates until your high and fortified walls, in which you trust, come down throughout all your land; and they shall besiege you at all your gates throughout all your land which the LORD your God has given you. You shall eat the fruit of your own body, the flesh of your sons and your daughters whom the LORD your God has given you, in the siege and desperate straits in which your enemy shall distress you. The sensitive and very refined man among you will be hostile toward his brother, toward the wife of his bosom, and toward the rest of his children whom he leaves behind, so that he will not give any of them the flesh of his children whom he will eat, because he has nothing left in the siege and desperate straits in which your enemy shall distress you at all your gates. The tender and delicate woman among you, who would not venture to set the sole of her foot on the ground because of her delicateness and sensitivity, will refuse to the husband of her bosom, and to her son and her daughter, her placenta which comes out from between her feet and her children whom she bears; for she will eat them secretly for lack of everything in the siege and desperate straits in which your enemy shall distress you at all your gates. If you do not carefully observe all the words of this law that are written in this book, that you may fear this glorious and awesome name, THE LORD YOUR GOD, then the LORD will bring upon you and your descendants extraordinary plagues—great and prolonged plagues— and serious and prolonged sicknesses. (Deuteronomy 28:15–59)

As you can see, when God sets His mind to chasten, punish, judge, and destroy, He gives a nation no hiding place. Nothing is beyond His reach, no cherished arena outside His wrath.

And in case you are wondering, every single threat just mentioned was carried out against Judah, Israel, the Canaanite nations, the Babylonians, and nations throughout history. We are no better than they were; we are not exempt from the sovereign rule of God.

Is America doomed? Is there no hope? Can we mitigate the sentence by some act of contrition and repentance on our part?

We are going to be judged. There is no way around it. The judgment has already begun. The question is, how severe will the judgment get? And, will we survive?

In the Bible, the Ten Northern Tribes—Israel—were judged and scattered, never restored. Yet the Two Southern Tribes—Judah and Benjamin—were judged and then restored.

In Nineveh Jonah preached imminent doom, yet God spared them (see Jonah 3). But one hundred years later, when Nahum announced their destruction, no repentance came forth and hence no such stay of execution from heaven came forth (see the book of Nahum).

Why? What saved Judah? What saved Nineveh the first time? What can save us?

Repentance.

May our eyes run with tears. May we ammend our ways. And may God see from Heaven and have mercy on us.

May we repent before it is too late.